בס״ד

To Know
and
To Care

An Anthology of Chassidic Stories
about the
Lubavitcher Rebbe שליט״א
Rabbi Menachem M. Schneerson

by Eliyahu and Malka Touger

Published by:
Sichos In English
788 Eastern Parkway • Brooklyn, New York 11213
(718) 778-5436 • Fax (718) 735-4139

TO KNOW AND TO CARE

Published and Copyrighted by
SICHOS IN ENGLISH
788 Eastern Parkway • Brooklyn, N.Y. 11213
Tel. (718) 778-5436

ISBN 1-8814-0003-4

5754 • 1993

Acknowledgments:
David Grossman and Uri Kaploun for copy-editing
Yosef Yitzchok Turner for layout and typography
Yonah Avtzon for countless hours of painstaking effort
in making this dream a reality.

Table of Contents

Introduction —
Of Rebbes and Stories

It was about two o'clock in the morning, and the chassidic mentor and his young students had been sharing several earnest hours of candid soul-searching around a long table at a *farbrengen*. As happens, the formalities of the early part of the gathering began to fall away. The melodies they were singing together became imperceptibly slower, deeper and more intense. The tone of the discussion likewise turned from the theoretical to the personal.

Reb Yoel Kahan, the elder chassid leading the gathering, turned to one of his students and quietly asked, "Nu, Yossel? How many Rebbes do you have?"

The student did not understand. Without minimizing the importance of any other contemporary *tzaddikim*, it is axiomatic in every chassidic group that a chassid has one Rebbe, one spiritual guide whom he has chosen to direct his personal growth.

After pausing to let his question sink in, Reb Yoel continued: "The Rebbe is a Rabbinic scholar *par excellence*; look at his studies of the *Talmud*. He is acclaimed as the generation's master in *nistar*, the mystical dimension of Torah study. He has introduced a new perspective on the study of *Rashi*, showing how his commentaries reflect the simple meaning of the Torah. His is the address to which tens of thousands turn for a blessing when they are in need, and he is a leader who takes a stance on political matters in *Eretz Yisrael* and elsewhere. And you can go on and on. Now how many Rebbeim do you have?

"Do you consider all of these as different qualities? Or can you perceive something deeper, a comprehensive thrust that unites all these different dimensions? Can you see all the Rebbe's different accomplishments as reflecting a single whole?"

* * *

With Reb Yoel's insight in mind, the stories contained in this book reveal a multi-dimensional picture of the Rebbe's leadership, showing many different perspectives of his personality. Our intent, however, is also to communicate something more than what is being said, to intimate to our readers an awareness of the general thrust that runs through all these different narratives.

Giving sole focus to any particular aspect of the Rebbe's personality, for example, the miracles that he works, the advice he gives people, his scholarship, narrows — and in that way, distorts — the picture of the Rebbe we all have.

Every person who has developed a relationship with the Rebbe *Shlita* has his own way of talking about him. But every person also realizes that his viewpoint is only a limited one and that there is something much greater about the Rebbe that he cannot describe. Nevertheless, by seeing a variety of these personal perspectives, it is possible to develop a heightened sensitivity to what that greater dimension is.

It is our feeling that stories express this best. Stories are alive. In contrast to a biography, which may often represent an academic perspective on a person's life, in stories his responses to the people and the circumstances he encounters breathe with vitality. Besides, biographies come with explicit or implied conclusions; stories quietly allow the reader to draw his own.

Storytelling is an age-old chassidic practice. The Rebbeim of *Chabad* would refer to chassidic stories as the *Torah Shebichsav* (the Written Law) of *Chassidus*. That name is significant, for chassidic stories, like the stories of the Patriarchs, Moshe Rabbeinu, and the other heroes of the *Tanach*, are "living Torah," expressions of infinite G-dly truth. Moreover, these truths are not expressed as theoretical principles, but as events occurring within the real-life framework of day-to-day experience.

In this vein, the question has frequently been asked: Why doesn't the *Talmud* include a tractate devoted to the subject of the love and fear of G-d? Chassidim would answer that this is unnecessary. The *tzaddikim,* the righteous sages of every generation, provide us with firsthand experience of these qualities, and hence there is no need to have recourse to a mere academic treatment of the subject.

Similarly, our Sages note[1] that the prophet Elisha is praised for "pouring water over the hands of Eliyahu,"[2] and explain that sharing in the day-to-day life of a sage is even more instructive than studying with him. For it is through seeing a Torah leader's response to actual life experiences that we can plumb his inner depth and appreciate the direction and purpose with which he endows others. This kind of perception is shared through stories.

* * *

In some circles, chassidic stories are considered to belong somewhere in history. Yes, such things would happen, but in the past. In the ongoing Lubavitch tradition, chassidic storytelling is and was always a fusion of past and present, because new chassidic stories are continually taking place. Publishing this collection of stories is intended to reinforce this conception of ongoing activity, for stories show life, and one of the signs of life is continuous growth and movement.

This is of course not intended to be a complete collection of the stories told about the Rebbe *Shlita.* This is impossible, because as mentioned before new stories are always happening, and moreover the number of stories concerning the Rebbe would fill many volumes the size of this one. We have chosen these stories, because we feel that they contain a lesson or a directive that a reader can apply in his divine service.

* * *

The Kotzker Rebbe was wont to say, "Anyone who believes that all the stories ever told about the Baal Shem Tov actually happened is a fool. At the same time, anyone who says that it

---

1.   *Berachos* 7b.
2.   *II Kings* 3:11.

is impossible for any particular story to have taken place is a non-believer, for nothing is beyond the potential of a *tzaddik*."

In other words, there are inconsistencies and contradictions between one story about the Baal Shem Tov and others, so that it is impossible for all of these stories to have actually occurred. Nevertheless, every one of the stories, no matter how wondrous the miracles involved, could have transpired. For a *tzaddik* is uniquely able to reveal a level of spirituality that transcends the natural order.

The above adage can be applied, not only to the stories of the Baal Shem Tov, but to those involving his spiritual heirs, the chassidic Rebbeim who have continued his tradition until the present day. Since these stories have been mainly communicated by word of mouth, some particulars could have been embellished or omitted by one of the tellers, or forgotten by a listener. Nevertheless, the germ of each story, the spiritual message which it intended to convey, remained intact.

In regard to the stories recounted in this series, we have endeavored to minimize the number of inaccuracies, trying to present the details of the stories as they took place. With this intent, we have tried to check these particulars with the people involved, or at the very least, with those who heard the stories from them.

Nevertheless, when it was impossible to contact the principals, we have occasionally had to rely on second- and even third-hand narratives, and thus there is a possibility of minor inaccuracies creeping in.

* * *

Two years ago, this introduction would have ended here. At present, there is a further point which must be clarified. And, in the time-honored tradition of chassidim, we have chosen to do so via the medium of a story.

It so happens that the exchange rate of the Israeli shekel is established by the government according to the American dollar. When the dollar is strong, the shekel can be drastically devalued and in one moment, its worth *vis-à-vis* the dollar can change by several per cent. In regard to European currency, by contrast, the fluctuations of the shekel are more gradual.

One of the diamond merchants in the main diamond exchange in Ramat Gan, Israel, buys diamonds in Israel with American dollars. He then travels to Europe and sells them for European currency with which he returns to Israel and changes into dollars or shekels.

Once this merchant bought diamonds for dollars in Israel and sold them in Europe, returning home to Israel satisfied with his transactions. Suddenly, however, it became clear that although his actual sales had been successful, he was going to lose money on the deal. The dollar had risen sharply and the European currency he was now holding had lost a tremendous amount of its original value. What had been a comfortable profit was now a minor loss.

He didn't know how to proceed. His logic told him to accept the loss, buy dollars with his European currency despite the high rate, and proceed further. But his heart told him that maybe he would be making a mistake. Although he was not a Lubavitcher chassid, he was experienced enough in his relationship with the Rebbe to know the address to which to turn in a time of doubt.

The dealer relayed his question to a *Chabad* emissary in Kiryat Gat who in turn, called the Rebbe's office. Within hours, the Rebbe gave his answer; not to buy dollars.

On that very same day, one of the merchant's friends also went to the diamond exchange on his return from Europe. He found himself in the very same situation; he too had made a profit on diamonds in Europe, but now had lost money due to the change in the exchange rate.

When his friend heard about the Rebbe's answer, he asked the dealer, "Is this advice for everyone or just for you?" The dealer didn't know what to reply, so the friend picked up the telephone and asked the Rebbe's secretary to submit the same question again, but with his own name.

Shortly afterwards, together with the Rebbe's other mail, the secretary submitted this question. This time, only a few hours after the previous answer, the Rebbe gave instructions for the person to buy dollars.

The jewelry merchant was confused when he heard the answer: "Didn't the Rebbe just instruct my friend a few hours ago not to buy dollars?"

"That's right," answered the secretary. "But now the Rebbe is telling you to buy dollars."

A few weeks later, the first diamond dealer called the Rebbe's secretary and told him: "I waited until the dollar dropped once more. Thank G-d, I was able to convert my European currency into dollars with a sizable profit.

"My friend followed the Rebbe's directive and exchanged the currency for dollars immediately. On the very next day, someone approached him with a solid business venture which required immediate cash; he would accept only dollars, no other currency. My friend joined in, and profited greatly. Had he not had the dollars in his possession, he would have lost the opportunity!"

This story happened several months ago, in the fall of the previous year (5753/1993).

The Rebbe remains the Rebbe. Countless people from all over the world continue to turn to him with questions regarding their spiritual and material concerns. And they receive answers. The stories that are recorded in the pages that follow are not merely past history: they are part of an ongoing present. Indeed, the Rebbe's secretaries report that the volume of mail the Rebbe receives has increased in the last year. More people from all over the world are turning to him. And the answers they receive encourage them to write again and again.

May the vitality which the stories of the Rebbe *Shlita* generates in our divine service arouse Divine blessings which will bring him a complete and speedy recovery, and enable him to lead the entire Jewish people to the Redemption in the immediate future.

Eliyahu Touger

13 Tishrei, 5754

Chapter 1 —
Enhancing Achievement

Not long before his passing, Reb Zushya of
Anapoli told his disciples: "When I appear before the
heavenly court in judgment, they're not going to ask
me, 'Zushya, why weren't you as great as Abraham,
Isaac, or Jacob?' They're going to ask me, 'Zushya,
why weren't you Zushya? Why weren't you the best
Zushya you could possibly be?'"

* * *

This thrust — motivating every individual to use
his own capacities, whatever they may be, to the
utmost — has always characterized the relationship
the Rebbe has established with people from many
different walks of life. We have collected several
examples of various people whose relationship with
the Rebbe has escalated their potential for
achievement.

Professor Yirmeyahu (Herman) Branover has achieved world-wide renown as an authority on magneto-hydrodynamics. Research in this area of alternative energy technology is carried out by a very limited number of highly trained professionals. Raised in the then Soviet Union, Professor Branover's published research had won him an international reputation in this field in the '60s.

Along with his work on hydrodynamics, Professor Branover has a dynamic Jewish heart. He applied for an emigration visa to Israel, knowing that it would mark the end of his professional career in the Soviet Union. He was dismissed from his post at the Academy of Sciences in Riga and prevented from continuing his research.

During this time, he was exposed to the Torah and *mitzvos* by members of the Lubavitch *chassidic* underground. When he was finally allowed to emigrate from the Soviet Union to Israel in 1972, he was already fully observant.

After making *aliyah*, Professor Branover was in constant demand as a lecturer, but not only in his profession. He was frequently invited to lecture on science and Torah. Campus audiences around the globe were extremely interested to hear an internationally renowned scientist reconcile his belief in the Torah with the supposed conflicts emerging from modern science.

"In the winter of 1973," relates Professor Branover, "I was on a lecture tour in the United States. Towards the end of the two-month tour, Rabbi Avraham Shemtov, one of the leading *shluchim*, requested that I add the University of Pennsylvania to my itinerary. My wife and I were both weary from the constant travel, but our commitment to spread Torah motivated us to agree.

"Shortly before the scheduled date, I was privileged to visit the Rebbe *Shlita* at *yechidus* (a private meeting). Among other matters, I mentioned the trip to Philadelphia. The Rebbe inquired about the details of the program and commented:

'During your stay in Philadelphia, do not forget to introduce yourself to a local professor who has an interest in your field.'

"The Rebbe's statement baffled me. I was well acquainted with the names of the American scientists involved in magneto-hydrodynamics and I knew the universities with which they were associated. I was certain that no Philadelphian was familiar with my field.

"I made the trip to Philadelphia following the busy schedule of lectures. On the morning of my arrival, when Rabbi Shem Tov met me at the train station, I spoke about my encounter with the Rebbe. I mentioned the Rebbe's strange remark and added that it appeared to be an error.

"'The Rebbe does not make mistakes,' Rabbi Shemtov said emphatically. 'Allow me to assist you in locating the scientist.'

"Rabbi Shemtov convinced me to visit Temple University and the University of Pennsylvania and to check the faculties of these institutions. After many hours of searching, we were introduced to Professor Hsuan Yeh. It was a refreshing change of pace to engage in a sophisticated discussion with a person who was clearly knowledgeable in magneto-hydrodynamics.

As we concluded our conversation, Professor Yeh said: 'In six weeks there will be a Magneto-Hydrodynamic Energy Convention at Stanford University in California. Although the program is already finalized, I will insist that your name be added to the list of lecturers. A colleague who has arrived so recently from Russia should be given the opportunity to present his thoughts.'

"I looked at him in surprise. 'Didn't you just say that the program was finalized?'

Professor Yeh added with a smile, 'You see, I am on the program committee.'

"I appreciated the Professor's offer, and yet I graciously declined, explaining that both my wife and I were anxious to return to our home in Israel. The trip had already been extended more than we would have liked.

"I returned to New York and we prepared to return home. Just before leaving, I wrote the Rebbe a report of our trip to Philadelphia, mentioning my encounter with Professor Yeh. Once again, the Rebbe made an unexpected statement. He advised me to reschedule my plans and to accept the invitation, for the convention presented an important opportunity.

"My wife and I were taken by surprise by the Rebbe's response. Despite the need to rearrange our plans, we were acquainted enough with the Rebbe to value his advice. I called Professor Yeh, who was happy to arrange for me to deliver a lecture.

"The significance of my participation at the convention became clear very rapidly. I met two representatives of the Office of Naval Research in Virginia who had read about my work, and who were prepared to finance further research. They added, 'We understand that you want to establish your laboratory in Israel, and we are willing to provide you with funds for your work there.'

"As a result, I set up a laboratory in Beer Sheva, which has gained worldwide recognition for its magneto-hydrodynamics research. My contract with the Office of Naval Research was been renewed six times since that original grant. I could not have imagined at that point how valuable and far-reaching the Rebbe's advice had been. This year, 1993, marks twenty years since the Stanford convention. My project has just been awarded a 15-million dollar grant by the United States government to further research and development of this energy technology."

Professor Branover frequently briefs the Rebbe on his various research projects. In one report, he presented a very sophisticated study built upon extensive calculations that had been prepared by computer. As he reviewed the details, the Rebbe remarked: "Two numbers here are inconsistent."

Professor Branover was stunned. "But all the calculations were done by computer and the program used is based on our most advanced theory."

The Rebbe smiled. "With all due respect to the experts, you will see that there is an error."

In the preparation of the calculations, an incongruity indeed had appeared. It took Professor Branover's research team six months to locate it.

Once before Professor Branover was scheduled to address a conference of Jewish scientists, the Rebbe told him: "You have an important message to communicate. Tell your colleagues that as a scholar of solar energy you encourage every Jew to emulate the sun.

"Why is this star of such great importance? There are larger heavenly bodies, indeed, many which dwarf the sun in size. What is unique about the sun? It provides light and generates heat.

"There are other heavenly phenomena called black holes. These are also powerful sources of energy, but in this instance, the energy is directed inward. The black holes pull everything, even the energy they emit, to themselves.

"The sun, by contrast, generously gives of itself to the entire planetary system. So, too, a Jew must radiate *Ahavas Yisrael* — love for a fellow Jew. After all, if the sun was only capable of heating its own mass, who would have paid any attention to it?"

Professor Branover also is active in developing programs of Jewish education and professional training for Jews in the former Soviet Union and for Russian immigrants to *Eretz Yisrael*. In the course of these activities, he has been chosen by the Rebbe for several missions.

"In the spring of 1985, I received word from the Rebbe's office that the Rebbe requested to speak to me," relates Professor Branover. "Of course, I arrived at "770" as soon as I could.

The Rebbe greeted me and informed me of his desire that I relay his forthcoming message to various persons in Russia. Not in my wildest dreams was I prepared for the content of the message.

"The Rebbe unraveled before me the precise details of the unbelievable change that was going to take place in Russia. With Mikhail Gorbachev's ascent to power, a new era of openness and freedom would begin, the Rebbe prophesied. Waves of Russian Jews would immigrate to *Eretz Yisrael.* Two years afterwards, in expectation of this wave of immigration, the Rebbe initiated the plan to build a special housing project in Jerusalem for the new immigrants.

"To say that I was stunned is quite an understatement. If I had heard these words from anyone but the Rebbe, I would have dismissed them as fantasy. As such, I was neither surprised nor offended when various people in Russia whom I contacted by phone were skeptical. 'Are you sure this is exactly what the Rebbe said?' they asked again and again. And, may I add, these people were not unfamiliar with the Rebbe. Quite the contrary, these were his own people who were directing the Lubavitch underground activities in Russia. It was simply that the Rebbe's prediction seemed so far-fetched."

"In the spring of 1985, newspapers such as the *New York Times* and the *New York Post* had published front-page articles predicting that Gorbachev's government would follow a Communist hard line. This was felt even more powerfully by people who were living in the then Soviet Union.

"When I related the response from Russia to the Rebbe, he requested that I contact them once again, assuring them that these changes would indeed take place.

"The realization of the Rebbe's words is now history. In 1992, when Mikhail Gorbachev visited Israel, I was introduced to him, and I told him and his wife Rayisa what the Rebbe had said seven years earlier. Gorbachev was stunned. 'When I assumed power in 1987, I myself had no concrete plan for the future. I would like to meet this man who knew so much about the direction which my country and I would follow.'"

It is difficult to tell whether the business enterprises of Reb Yissachar Dov Weiss, a prominent West Coast businessman, support his charity endeavors or whether the distribution of charity sustains the business. Reb Yissachar Dov prefers the second explanation. "That is the real bottom line," he maintains. "Let me tell you about a friend also involved in business.

"This man had attempted several business ventures, but none of them had met with success. Once, he consulted the Rebbe before embarking on a new business. The Rebbe suggested that he give five thousand dollars to charity before starting the new position. The man was pressed for funds and failed to heed the Rebbe's advice. Shortly afterwards, his business faltered.

"Some time later, the man again presented his troubles to the Rebbe. 'I had advised you to give a substantial amount of money to charity,' the Rebbe reminded him. Saying this, he removed a volume of the Talmud from his shelf and read from it: 'Rabbi Yochanan teaches, *Aser bishvil shetisasher*' — "Tithe so that you may prosper."[1] Had you donated the money to charity, I would have been able to address a claim to Rabbi Yochanan....'

In another instance, Reb Yissachar Dov explained that "I have always wanted to fulfill my obligation to give charity properly. I was not always sure how much to give or which charity was the most deserving. I decided to consult with the Rebbe.

"The Rebbe responded: 'The most important thing is to give *tzedakah* with an open and happy heart. Take pen in hand,

---

1.   *Taanis* 9a.

and you will be able to sense the proper amount to write on the check.'

Having established such a relationship with the Rebbe, it is not surprising that Reb Yissachar Dov often consults him about his business affairs. "Once," Reb Yissachar Dov recalled, "I asked the Rebbe whether my company should go public on the stock market. 'One can make a fortune overnight,' I said with enthusiasm. 'This will enable me to donate a million dollars to Lubavitch institutions.'

"The Rebbe was less enthusiastic about my grandiose plans. After a short silence, he asked, 'Why would you want others to have a say in your business?'

"I was persistent, and ultimately, I received his blessing for the endeavor. Afterwards, the Rebbe asked: 'And what will you give me?' I responded spontaneously that I was willing to offer anything.

"'In that case,' the Rebbe replied, 'I would like you to give me a thousand pages of Talmudic study.'"

On many occasions the Rebbe's advice saved Reb Yissachar Dov from extensive losses. A favorite story involves an investment offer for Liberian diamonds on Africa's West Coast in 1976.

"The Belgian diamond dealers who had made the proposal were familiar with my business procedures," related Reb Yissachar Dov. "They knew that the Rebbe's blessing was essential to any of my endeavors. They were, however, surprised by the degree to which I relied upon him.

"'We understand that you want your Rebbe's blessing,' their representative remarked. 'After all, we are considering a million dollar project. But....'

"'Excuse me,' I cut him off. 'I will not invest anything before I receive the Rebbe's blessing and consent.'

"The jewelers were very anxious that I invest. 'We want to clarify your statement. Do you really mean that you will not take advantage of this opportunity unless the Rebbe approves? What does the Rebbe know about business or about African gems?'

"I did not answer. My past experience and burgeoning bank account had proven to me that the Rebbe's approval exceeded any calculable value.

"At my next opportunity, I discussed the subject with the Rebbe. He told me not to invest, warning me that a revolution was impendent.

"I was surprised. 'How's that?' I asked the Rebbe. 'Everybody in the business world knows that Liberia a neutral country, is the Switzerland of Africa.'

"The Rebbe was determined in his opinion: The political situation was shaky, and investment was dangerous. Anything longterm should not be considered at all. Only something where money can go in and out immediately was worth thinking about.

"The Belgian dealers were extremely disappointed and skeptical. 'A revolution in Liberia? The most stable country in Africa?'

"Soon afterwards, I invested fifty thousand dollars in the diamond business. I hired a broker, instructing him to purchase Liberian diamonds quickly and to depart immediately. He purchased coarse stones which were to be cut, polished, and then forwarded to the buyer.

"Shortly afterwards, the revolution which the Rebbe had predicted broke out. The stones were never exported, and I reclaimed only a portion of the price I paid. I comforted myself with the thought that I had not invested millions."

Rabbi Yitzchak Vorst is one of the dynamic forces behind Lubavitch activity in Holland. He is well suited to the job, because precise timing and calculated scheduling are ingrained in his Dutch culture. He has also been the recipient of numerous "timely" responses when corresponding with the Rebbe. It is obviously not a simple question of culture.

Rabbi Vorst relates, "World War II could not sever my family's seven-generation link with the Dutch Jewish community. After the trials and tribulations of the war, my father devoted himself to rebuilding Jewish life here, while at the same time urging the youth to emigrate to Israel. When I graduated as an engineer, I postponed my career, choosing to taste deeper Torah study. I enrolled in the Lubavitcher *Yeshivah* in Lod, Israel.

"During the spring, I spent the *yeshivah* break in the then small town of Ashdot Yam, by the sea. I learned that a new harbor was being built there. Considering my future, I inquired about possible employment at the project. My application was readily accepted. Having spent two months of study at the *yeshivah*, I desired to seek the Rebbe's advice and blessing before making a final decision and signing a contract.

"I wrote the Rebbe a letter, but I did not receive a response. I consulted with the *yeshivah's mashpia* — Rabbi Shlomo Chaim Keselman, who served as a spiritual mentor to the students. 'Perhaps the letter was lost in the mail,' he suggested. I wrote again. Still no reply. I asked Rabbi Keselman once again. With a thoughtful look, he responded, 'I think the Rebbe is waiting for you to decide for yourself whether you want to continue your *yeshivah* studies.'

I had already come to the conclusion that I should continue the course of study I had begun at *yeshivah*. So on Friday morning, I wrote the Rebbe of my decision. I went out to mail the letter, only to discover two days later that a letter for me had arrived from New York, posted before the Rebbe received my letter.

"The Rebbe's reply to my question was clear. He advised me to continue studying for at least two years. The letter was dated the 9th of *Elul*.

"After an inspiring year at *yeshivah* in Israel, I felt that it was time to travel to the States and see the Rebbe. Shortly after my arrival, I prepared myself for a private *yechidus*. My letter contained several questions and requests for blessings. I also included a note about my father ע"ה, the late chief Rabbi of Rotterdam, reiterating a previous requests that the Rebbe appoint an official *shaliach* to fill the urgent needs of the Dutch Jewish community. To date, my father had not received a reply.

"After responding to my personal questions, the Rebbe addressed himself to my father's request and said: 'I have not yet found the appropriate person who both desires and is capable of filling this position.' At this point, the Rebbe's eyes met mine, and he looked at me with a broad smile.

"Later, contemplating on this *yechidus*, I suspected that the Rebbe was hinting that I assume this responsibility. I decided to ask the Rebbe if this was his intention. The Rebbe's answer was short and to the point: 'Continue your studies.'

"Months passed, and I concentrated vigorously on my studies. Eventually, my visa rights were nearing expiry and I consulted the Rebbe again. I was debating whether to return to Israel or to extend my stay in the States.

"I did not receive an answer. Upon the advice of the Rebbe's secretary, Rabbi Hodakov, I wrote a second time. There was still no reply. But a month later I did receive the Rebbe's answer, which clearly indicated that I should return to help build the Dutch Jewish community. Wondering why this answer had been so long in coming, I glanced at the date of the reply. It was the 9th of Elul, exactly two years since that first reply which I had received while still studying in Israel: to continue studying for at least two years!

"While I was studying in New York, I had another experience with the Rebbe's 'expertise' in proper timing. I was twenty-five, and my friends and relatives had gently hinted that I consider marriage. I sought the Rebbe's advice. Instead of extending his usual blessing for this type of question, the

Rebbe responded, 'Do not pursue this matter at all until the end of the school year, or at least until after the holiday of Shavuos.'

"The answer surprised me. I wondered about the two dates which the Rebbe had mentioned. What did he mean by this response?

"Only later did I grasp the extent of this time frame. In Brunoy (near Paris), there is a well-known Lubavitch family called Kalmanson. Some time after I received the above answer from the Rebbe, their daughter considered a trip to the States. Her intention was two-fold; to see the Rebbe, and to inquire about a suitable match. She debated whether to spend the holiday of Shavuos in Crown Heights or to set her departure date for the end of the school year.

"That young woman later became my wife. It now became clear that the time when I was to begin acting on my future had depended upon the departure date on her Paris-New York plane ticket."

"Making a total commitment to a Lubavitch way of life was an ongoing process for me," explains Rabbi Nachman Meir Bernhard, Rabbi of the prestigious Oxford Synagogue in Johannesburg, South Africa. "Before I left America for South Africa, it was the Rebbe who, in a long first Yechidus in 1964, convinced me that I had a responsibility to return to the Rabbinate, although I had inclinations to the contrary, and he encouraged me to accept my present Rabbinic position.

"After ten more years of community service, I began to consider leaving the Rabbinate again. For many years, I had been longing to settle in *Eretz Yisrael*, and I felt that the time had come to make this dream a reality. I began making plans and scheduled a pilot trip in search of a suitable position and housing. I was involved enough in Lubavitch by that time to know that I should consult the Rebbe before making any binding decisions. So, after my visit to *Eretz Yisrael*, I flew to New York before returning to South Africa.

"It was the summer of 1974, and this was my second *yechidus* with the Rebbe. At great length, the Rebbe explained why I could accomplish much more by continuing to serve the South African Jewish community, 'Don't you think that I too would like to be there (in *Eretz Yisrael*), close to the *Kedushah* (Holiness)? But we have responsibilities.'

"Though I obviously said I would follow the Rebbe's directive, I could not hide my disappointment. I felt the need to discuss the matter further with the Rebbe before my return to South Africa, and I hesitantly requested to be allowed another *yechidus*. I was grateful when the Rebbe agreed to see me again on Sunday, for I knew this was most unusual.

"That *Shabbos*, the Rebbe granted me extraordinary measures of attention and encouragement. I appreciated this very much, and the first thing I said when I went into his study on Sunday was a word of thanks for the expression of closeness *(Keiruv)*.

"'Expressing closeness is a two-way street,' the Rebbe replied.

"'Must I too show closeness to the Rebbe?!' I asked in wonder.

"'Yes!'

"'What does the Rebbe mean? I have already agreed to accept the Rebbe's advice. I am staying in South Africa.'

"'Yes,' said the Rebbe, 'but your decision should not be made with the resignation of one who has reluctantly accepted a decree. Rather, it should come happily and good-heartedly!'

"Although I didn't move to *Eretz Yisrael*, over the years the Rebbe spoke to me on several occasions about issues concerning the Holy Land. Once he told me of a conversation he had with the then Minister of Defense of Israel. The Rebbe had asked him what plan or strategy the government had for the next ten years.

"The Minister answered, 'G-d will help.'

"'What's going on here?' the Rebbe said. 'I am asking you like a layman (i.e., from a worldly perspective), and you are answering me like a Rebbe!' He then grew very serious and said, 'The truth is, they have no plan!'

"The Rebbe has also expressed his opinion on South Africa's internal policies. On more than one occasion, he spoke of the need for the government to replace the apartheid regulations with a system of justice and equity. Upon the Rebbe's directive, Rabbi Lipskar, the head *shliach* in South Africa, and I once again visited a former Prime Minister, John Vorster, and encouraged him in his very cautious pioneering attempts to modify these policies, conveying the Rebbe's prophetic words that South Africa had a bright future.

"Some months later, we received notice from government officials that the Prime Minister requested to see us again. This was just a short time before a scheduled historic meeting in Europe with U.S. Secretary of State, Henry Kissinger, which the South African government regarded as vital to the country's future.

"After welcoming us, the Prime Minister lost no time in expressing his desire: 'I would like to know what the Gentleman in New York has to say now.' This was just one of many indications that innumerable Jews and Gentiles have drawn great comfort from the Rebbe's repeated reassurances that all will be well in South Africa — and that there is no need to fear, panic or flee.

On a more personal note, Rabbi Bernhard recalls one of numerous occasions when the Rebbe assisted him with regard to his family. "Once, during *yechidus*, I mentioned that one of my daughters who had been an excellent student was becoming lax and falling behind in her studies. The Rebbe listened attentively and said, 'This is not laziness. She has a particular medical problem', which he named. 'Your wife should take her to a specialist, who will find and treat the condition.'

"After the *yechidus*, I immediately phoned my wife. She took our daughter to see a specialist, who arrived at the same diagnosis, and prescribed effective treatment."

"For the past twenty-odd years, since I had first met the Rebbe, my life can be described as a pocket full of miracles," says Mr. David Chase, one of America's foremost businessmen. "And I don't mean only in my business endeavors. To the contrary, the greatest miracle of them may have been my ability to appreciate the message that the Rebbe conveys. My relationship with the Rebbe has given me and many others a sensitivity to matters which are beyond ordinary mortal understanding. For this reason, over the years, I have committed myself to advancing the Rebbe's work in many areas and to different people.

"The Rebbe's directives are so far-reaching and never ending. The Rebbe himself once described his 'insatiable appetite' for ongoing Jewish activity. Perhaps it is the Rebbe's total lack of self-concern and constant devotion to the welfare of others that has motivated me to regard my Lubavitch activity as a cherished labor of love.

"Once, at the annual meeting of the Machne Israel Development Fund, I told the Rebbe how pleased I was to be one of the soldiers in his army.

"You are not merely a soldier," the Rebbe replied. "You are my general."

"Some time later, when I came to receive a dollar on Sunday, I received a promotion; the Rebbe told me, "I regard you as a five-star general."

"I consider it my pleasure and duty to help others benefit from an association with the Rebbe, just as I have benefited in both my business and private life. My activities bring me in contact with many public figures around the world, and I do not hesitate to share my experiences with the Rebbe and with his directives with Jews and non-Jews.

"I often visit my native land, Poland, where I have business interests. Prior to one trip to Poland, I visited New York and asked for the Rebbe's blessing. The Rebbe handed me an additional dollar, saying: "Give this to a person in Poland who will benefit the Jewish people."

"Due to my business endeavors, I have various contacts in the Polish government, and I contemplated who would be the proper recipient of the Rebbe's dollar. One day I found myself aboard a domestic flight with the newly elected President Lech Walesa. I had several contacts with Mr. Walesa in the past, and it occurred to me that I would not be able to find a better person to whom to give the Rebbe's dollar. I approached him, handed him the dollar, and conveyed the Rebbe's message.

"Mr. Walesa looked at me thoughtfully. "I sincerely hope I will be able to live up to your Rebbe's expectation."

"After this encounter, my acquaintance with Mr. Walesa grew and we became quite friendly. Some time later, Mr. Walesa personally invited me to accompany him on his upcoming visit to Israel. This trip was a major breakthrough in relations between the two countries, and he felt that my inclusion in his delegation would be helpful.

"Though I was not inclined to accept the invitation, I saw this as a further step in enhancing the impact of the Rebbe's influence on 'a person who will benefit the Jewish people,' and I agreed. Mr. Walesa told me he wanted to express the regret of the Polish people for their inexcusable behavior towards the Jews during World War II.

"As a Holocaust survivor myself, I insisted that his statement be forthright, without minimizing the issue or covering it up with bland diplomatic wording.

"Mr. Walesa surprised the Israeli government with his non-evasive statement of regret on behalf of the Polish people. Subsequently, former Prime Minister Shamir was very demanding in several points, including a change in the pro-Arab approach that had been advocated by Poland's previous Communist leaders and a cessation of arms sales to countries hostile to Israel. Despite Poland's heavy financial loss, one could almost see the Rebbe's directive at work as Mr. Walesa agreed to one concession after another.

"Later, I accompanied him on a visit to the Diaspora Museum, where I pointed out the picture of the Rebbe which is displayed there. "Is this my Rebbe?" Mr. Walesa asked bowing his head in reverence. Mr. Walesa's response was striking. He was clearly impressed and moved by the Rebbe's intense gaze. He actually lowered his head as if acknowledging his leadership.

"In many other instances, I have been privileged to bring the Rebbe's message to people who might otherwise not have been exposed to them. The best way we can reciprocate for the good which the Rebbe showers upon us is to express his teachings, ideals, and principles in our daily lives."

Great Torah giants of our day stand in awe before the magnitude of the all-encompassing knowledge of Torah texts and sources which the Rebbe displays in all realms and levels of study. The illustrious Rabbi Yisrael Yitzchak Piekarski, *Rosh Yeshivah* in Lubavitch for many years, said: "Appreciation of the Rebbe's unparalleled knowledge of Torah takes priority over describing his miraculous feats. Nevertheless, there is a connection between the two. If I am not mistaken, the Rebbe himself once said, 'One who is great in the study of Torah law *(nigleh)* is also great in other things.'"

His preference for highlighting the Rebbe's scholarship did not, however, prevent Rabbi Piekarski from relating some of his own personal experiences with the Rebbe. "Once, prior to a journey, I visited the Rebbe. When I informed him of the details of my return flight, he responded, 'Why should you stay away so long? You can return two days earlier.' I was very surprised. I had already made all the arrangements and booked my flight. The departure date fitted my itinerary perfectly.

"Of course, I did not question the Rebbe's remark, and immediately changed my plans. Later, I learned that the flight on which I was originally scheduled to depart met with disaster. The plane was involved in a tragic accident in Bulgaria and its passengers perished.

"And yet," continued Rabbi Piekarski, "perhaps more than these miracles, is the tremendous concern for others that the Rebbe displays. His willingness to deal with the most insignificant and minute details touches me most deeply.

"Before my annual summer trip, the Rebbe always asks about my itinerary and the length of my stay in each country. He always gives me *shaliach mitzvah*[2] coins in the currency of the countries I will visit. As a rule, Switzerland is usually my first stop.

"Once, the Rebbe spent a considerable amount of time searching his drawers for Swiss coins. Waiting uncomfortably, I finally said that the Swiss accept U.S. coins as well. Only then did the Rebbe seem satisfied and stop his search.

"On another occasion, shortly before the wedding of a certain *yeshivah* student of limited means, the Rebbe questioned me in detail about the wedding arrangements. I could

---

2.   It is customary to give a traveler some money to give to charity in the course of his journey. This designates him as a *shaliach* ("emissary") charged with a *mitzvah*. Our Sages *(Pesachim* 8a) declare: "A person who is on a mission to perform a *mitzvah* will not be harmed."

not understand how the Rebbe knew of all these minute details, nor could I understand his concern. The Rebbe noticed my discomfort in discussing these details and explained, 'I manage the distribution of funds from several charities. This is a responsibility that I don't want to give up.'"

A colorful combination of adept professionalism, personal charm and downright *chutzpah* blended in the "770" photographer, Reb Levi Yitzchak Frieden.

Reb Levi Itche, as he was affectionately called, has visited "770" from his home in *Eretz Yisrael* during each of the High Holidays since 1975. His camera's lens captured many touching incidents, such as the Rebbe's blessing of *yeshivah* students moments before Yom Kippur began. With one eye on his watch, as he dared not desecrate the holiest day of the year, and the other eye focusing his camera, Levi Itche took shot after shot of this memorable moment.

He was so involved in his work that the Rebbe once told Frieden to tell the *yeshivah* students studying at "770" that if their enthusiasm would match Frieden's passion for photography, things would look much better.

Frieden was eager to share the scenes of "770" with other Jews in *Eretz Yisrael*. In 1976, he held an exhibit called "770" at Tel Aviv's journalist center, Beit Sokolov. The exhibit, which later moved to Jerusalem and Bar Ilan University, afforded the large crowd of viewers a mix of spiritual experience and professional expertise.

On the whole, the exhibit was highly applauded. However, one journalist commented in the guest book: 'With all due respect to the superb photography, the subject you have chosen is extremely clerical and takes us back to the primitive darkness of the Middle Ages.'

"Upon my next visit to the States," Frieden continued. "I presented the Rebbe with the guest book. Leafing through it quickly, the Rebbe noticed that negative remark. "'Please compliment the journalist on his strength of character. It takes fortitude to differ from all of the other responses,' the Rebbe said, 'But tell him that not everything in the Middle Ages was dark. Furthermore, ask him to review his own newspaper. Today's news is not all that bright either.'

"The Rebbe then handed me a dollar, asking me to deliver it to that journalist."

Before he returned to *Eretz Yisrael* each year, Reb Levi Itche waited at the sidewalk before the Rebbe's home to take leave of the Rebbe. He always thanked the Rebbe for allowing him to take photographs, excused himself for any disturbance he may have caused, and also asked for a blessing for his family.

One year, he waited with increased emotion. He had just met a young man who sorrowfully confided of his distress at having been married ten years without having children. "You have your own way of approaching the Rebbe. Please mention my difficulty," he asked. Reb Levi Itche was touched by his request and resolved to bring up the subject in his brief encounter with the Rebbe.

As he described the man's troubles, the Rebbe gazed sternly at Reb Levi Itche while the secretary, Rabbi Binyamin Klein, waited nearby to drive the Rebbe to "770". When Frieden concluded, the Rebbe responded: "Tell the young man to write a note with his name, his wife's name and the names of their mothers. I will take it to the Previous Rebbe's grave."[3]

Then, as he often did, the Rebbe invited Reb Levi Itche to accompany him in the car to "770". Usually, Reb Levi Itche would decline. However, this time he entered the car, hoping to put in another good word for the young man. He did not

---

3.   The holy place at which the Rebbe reads the names of those who have asked him to intercede on their behalf.

have the opportunity. During the short ride, the Rebbe asked Frieden about his family and inquired if he had purchased a gift for his wife and children.

When the car arrived at "770", Frieden took leave of the Rebbe and rushed to the man's home. He quickly gave him the Rebbe's response, took off for the airport and boarded his plane to Israel.

Less than a year later, on the twenty-fifth of Elul, Frieden returned to New York. As he arrived in Crown Heights, his host, Rabbi Gavriel Shapiro, was just leaving his house. "Welcome, Reb Levi Itche. Remember when you requested a blessing for that childless couple at the beginning of the year? Well, you're just in time for the *bris.*"

Frieden glanced at his watch. It was almost 10 o'clock, when the Rebbe would be leaving his home for "770". Without a second thought, he dashed over to President St. "Rebbe," said Frieden, "the blessing you gave last fall was fulfilled. Today is the *bris.*"

The Rebbe listened patiently, radiating composure. "Don't make an issue of everything," he said waving his hand in dismissal. "There is no need for you to get excited."

Chapter 2 —
The Concerns of This World

At the turn of the century, Reb Shmuel Gourary
was a successful businessman whose enterprises
brought him into contact with many chassidim from
Poland and Galicia. Once after a contract was
negotiated, he and a group of several chassidim,
each following a different Rebbe, sat down to talk.
Each told a story of a miracle his Rebbe had
performed.

The other chassidim had impressive stories,
relating how their Rebbeim had helped heal the
sick, bless the childless with offspring, and bring
about financial success. When Reb Shmuel's turn
came, he told about an investment he had made in
the forests of Russia. He had hesitated to make the
investment, for a substantial sum was required and
there was a great risk that the onset of the Russian
winter would delay the timber from ever reaching its
destination downstream. On the other hand, he
stood to make a hefty profit. He consulted the
Rebbe Rashab who told him to go ahead and invest.

From the beginning, problems began to arise:
the cost of labor rose, and the quality of timber was
not as high as expected. On several occasions Reb

Shmuel asked the Rebbe if perhaps he should pull out, accept whatever losses he had suffered, but still save something. Each time, the Rebbe told him to persevere. Finally, as they were preparing to ship the logs downriver, a cold spell hit and the river froze. That was the end; by the spring, the timber would be almost useless.

"So what's the miracle?" Reb Shmuel's listeners asked. "The miracle is," he replied, "that I remained a chassid. I trust the Rebbe and know that this was for my own good. Had this happened to any one of you, you would probably have gone looking for a new Rebbe."

* * *

In *Chabad,* the connection with a Rebbe is an all-encompassing one. It does not depend on "what the Rebbe has done for me," but is rather a deep, inner bond, based on the realization that the Rebbe can guide every facet of a person's spiritual development. On the other hand, the tangible benefits that often result from a connection with the Rebbe cannot be ignored.

Mr. Jeffrey Kimball, a lawyer and an active member of the Lubavitch community in Springfield, Mass., weighed the offer. Although it was no small investment, the profits seemed so secure that the banks had offered to lend him the 15 million dollars required without guarantors. Nevertheless, Mr. Kimball valued the Rebbe's advice. Before signing the contract, he asked for a blessing.

The Rebbe's reply consisted of two lengthy pages discussing the importance of adhering to a Torah lifestyle. "A Jew who fulfills G-d's commandments," the Rebbe wrote, will merit Divine blessings for success in all his endeavors. At the bottom of the letter, after his signature, the Rebbe added a postscript: "Regarding the business offer — it is not advisable."

Mr. Kimball had his answer. Now it was his associates' turn to ponder. How could he possibly turn down such a sound enterprise? Despite their insistence, Mr. Kimball trusted the Rebbe and did not make the investment.

Two years later, the soundness of the Rebbe's reply became openly apparent. Mr. Kimball had been asked to make a long-term investment in Nicaragua. Despite the country's previous stability, its government had been overthrown by Communist rebels and many foreign investments were nationalized.

"Sounds like a decent offer," mused Mr. Aharonson as he reached for the phone. A carpenter had advertised his workshop in the "For Sale" section of a local paper.

Shortly after an initial conversation, the two men met to discuss the details. The potential buyer and the seller were both eager to cut a deal, and they soon felt ready to draw up a contract.

"I've made an appointment with the lawyer for tomorrow at 10 o'clock," said the carpenter as he stood up.

He extended his hand to Mr. Aharonson, who shook it warmly, but added: "No, tomorrow is too soon. Although I'm very interested, I want to handle one more detail. You see, I always ask the Lubavitcher Rebbe for his consent and blessing before confirming any business transaction."

Although such an approach is common among the Rebbe's followers, it was strange to the carpenter. He agreed, but with some hesitation. "I respect your faith," he answered, "but please do not delay too long. After all, I do have other prospective buyers."

A few days later, the carpenter received a phone call. "I'm sorry," said Mr. Aharonson. "I am canceling my offer. The Rebbe implied that the deal is not for me."

The next day, a fire destroyed the carpentry. However, the financial loss was not as bad as it might have been had the transaction actually taken place.

The carpentry had been insured by its original owner. Thus, he suffered no major loss. As a matter of fact, he received more money from the insurance than he would have received from the sale. Mr. Aharonson, on the other hand, would not have been covered by this policy.

The Rebbe's advice thus proved beneficial to both the buyer and the seller — in a transaction that never took place.

"I cannot understand why I still have not received the Rebbe's blessing for this trip," Rabbi Nemes mused to himself nervously. He sells stamps and his dealings bring him into contact with postal authorities and private collectors in Central America. He would regularly visit Nicaragua in the winter and had already scheduled his appointments for this year's trip. As always, before finalizing his journey, he wrote to the Rebbe for a blessing. But instead of receiving an immediate answer, this time he had to wait for a reply.

As the date of his departure came near, Rabbi Nemes asked one of the Rebbe's secretaries to help him. After speaking with the Rebbe, the secretary asked Rabbi Nemes for a detailed itinerary of the trip. When Rabbi Nemes forwarded the information to the Rebbe, the Rebbe responded: "Make the trip — but not at present."

Rabbi Nemes found it difficult to comprehend the Rebbe's advice. 'This is the most profitable season for purchasing stamps,' he thought. 'Moreover, I have already arranged meetings with prominent dealers. And postponing this trip will complicate the other journeys I had planned. I cannot understand this; the Rebbe has never suggested a change in my plans before.'

Nevertheless, the Rebbe's followers are not deterred simply because they don't comprehend his advice. Rabbi Nemes postponed his trip and canceled his appointments.

One need not be a devout believer in Divine Providence to appreciate the immense sense of relief felt by Rabbi Nemes and his family when they heard the shocking news that weekend. A severe earthquake had struck Managua, Nicaragua's capital, causing thousands of casualties and tremendous damage. "And I had been booked in a downtown hotel there," Rabbi Nemes thought with a shudder.

As time passed and the airport at Managua opened again to commercial traffic, Rabbi Nemes considered making his journey. His family was apprehensive. "The city is still plagued with widespread theft and plundering," they argued. But Rabbi Nemes felt optimistic. "The Rebbe did not disapprove of the trip entirely," he told them. "He merely suggested that I postpone it." Rabbi Nemes was further encouraged by the Rebbe's prompt blessing to reschedule the trip.

Rabbi Nemes was not prepared for the vast destruction in the streets of Managua. Collapsed buildings and mounds of rubble littered the city. Countless homeless wandered aimlessly, making its familiar districts seem foreign even to a frequent visitor.

With great difficulty and anxiety, Rabbi Nemes made his way to the Central Post Office. In contrast to his somber expectations, he was astounded to find the huge building standing erect, almost untouched by the earthquake. Quickening his step, he proceeded to the room of an official with whom he often did business.

As he opened the door, the official jumped up with a start. "Goodness! What a surprise!" he exclaimed with delight. "I hadn't expected any stamp dealer to come here now!"

After a friendly exchange, Rabbi Nemes began to talk business. However, the local man stopped him. "As you see, the city is in a state of upheaval. It will be some time until it is rebuilt. The stamp business is obviously not an immediate priority. You are a trustworthy dealer and we've always worked well together. Help yourself to any stamps you require. We'll be in touch about the price and payment schedule at a future date."

"That trip to Nicaragua was the most profitable I have ever made," concluded Rabbi Nemes.

"Let me tell you of a personal experience I had," began the young man from Antwerp. "I had been studying at *Yeshivas Kol Torah* in Jerusalem when my father fell ill. The ever-rising medical bills and prolonged absence from work drained our family's resources. I was compelled to leave my studies and go into business to help shoulder the burden.

"An acquaintance suggested that I write to the Lubavitcher Rebbe and request his blessing. I was only too happy to do so, green as I was in the business world. In his response, the Rebbe advised me to buy as many shares of a particular stock as possible the following Sunday.

"I followed the Rebbe's advice, although that particular stock did not seem to have any particular promise. Two days later, the price of these stocks unexpectedly soared. I immediately sold my shares, netting a very handsome profit."

A chassid of the Sadigora Rebbe joined the line to receive a dollar from the Rebbe one Sunday. He had been given an attractive offer to purchase a bakery, but was not sure what to do. He had difficulty contacting his own Rebbe and the owner of the bakery was pressing for an answer. When the chassid asked the Rebbe about the proposition, the Rebbe replied: "Why ask me? Ask a Rabbi from Cleveland."

The Sadigora chassid was bewildered at this strange reply, and left "770" puzzled and unsure of the course of action he should take. As it happened, he met an elderly couple on the way to his car and offered to give them a lift. In the course of conversation, the man introduced himself as a Rabbi from Cleveland.

The chassid immediately asked their advice regarding the purchase of the bakery. If this unusual turn of events seemed incredible, the chassid was further shocked to learn that the couple was related to the owners of the bakery.

"Since you asked," said the Rabbi's wife, "I'll tell you. The owner of the bakery is a decent fellow, but his business faltered because the workers are not trustworthy."

The Sadigora chassid had his answer. The contract of sale had included a clause requiring the purchaser to continue to employ the present staff. Needless to say, he did not purchase the bakery.

Chapter 3 —
Borrowed Resources

In selecting the stories for this book, we had to define what is a story about the Rebbe and what is a story about one of his chassidim. Often the Rebbe gives a single directive or a blessing, and everything else in the narrative was accomplished by a chassid.

Why then do we consider this a story about the Rebbe? — Because the chassid will tell you that he would not have been able to achieve what he accomplished on his own power; he relied the Rebbe's influence.

The nature of this dynamic of empowerment requires explanation. Often we see one or two Lubavitch *shluchim* begin activities in a city and, despite limited human and financial resources, within a short time, they bring about a heightening of Jewish consciousness. If you ask the young emissary how he was able to accomplish what he did, he will tell you in homely Yiddish, *"Mit der Rebbe's kochos"* ("With the Rebbe's power").

What does he mean? When we look up to someone with well-earned respect and feel that he genuinely knows us and believes in us, it is natural to want to live up to his expectations. With a pride that goes much deeper than self, we apply ourselves to the tasks before us with the intent of giving shape and form to the ideal we share. And we achieve far more than we ever might have dreamed of.

That can be readily understood. In addition, there is a Yiddish adage which says, "When G-d wants, even a broom can shoot." When a person thinks of himself as no more than a broom, and while not shirking responsibility, does not rely on his own unaided power, he opens himself up to a greater force. He becomes aware that something much larger than himself is working through him. And this is what the *shluchim* mean when they attribute their success to the Rebbe.

This dynamic of empowerment is not restricted to any exclusive group. On several occasions the Rebbe *Shlita* has explained that everyone is a *shaliach* — in his home, in his workplace, and in his environment — to use whatever potentials he has to spread the awareness and the observance of Jewish values.

Rabbi Dov Ber Levy, founder of O.K. Kashrus Laboratories, traveled throughout the world to help the international food industries maintain the laws of *kashrus*. During the course of these travels, he was charged by the Rebbe with various missions.

Rabbi Levy was invited to Russia during the pre-*perestroika* era to arrange kosher supervision for certain products the Russians desired to export. While involved in these activities, he also devoted himself to providing "soul food" for Russian Jewry.

The underground Lubavitch activity in Russia had produced a large number of Russian chassidim who felt close to the Rebbe, despite the fact that they were 6,000 miles away and had never met him in person. Rabbi Levy took a video camera with him and filmed these Russian Jews in what could be described as a private *yechidus* with the Rebbe. The Russian Jews would each face the camera and address the Rebbe as if they were speaking to him in person. On his return to New York, Rabbi Levy would play back the video recording for the Rebbe.[1]

On other travels, Rabbi Levy carried out various missions for the Rebbe. While some of the goals were explicit, Rabbi Levy sometimes felt that he was serving as a catalyst to fulfill an unspecified purpose.

Once, he had scheduled a trip to the Philippines to inspect a factory which produced food products for the international market. After planning his itinerary, he told the Rebbe about his upcoming trip and asked for a blessing.

The Rebbe replied with blessings for success, supplementing his good wishes with several dollars for *shaliach mitzvah gelt*.

---

1. At times the eve of December 25th was chosen for the showing, for this is a night when it is customary not to study Torah. See *Sefer Minhagim* (English translation, Kehot, N.Y., 1991), p. 162.

[It is customary to give a traveler some money to give to charity in the course of his journey. This designates him as a *shaliach* ("emissary") charged with a *mitzvah*. Our Sages declare:[2] "A person who is on a mission to perform a *mitzvah* will not be harmed." Thus, even if he encounters a dangerous situation on the journey, the person will merit protection.]

This time, the Rebbe added an instruction to the money which he included with his blessing — to visit and address the Philippine Jewish community, and to give them a donation of one hundred and eighty dollars on his behalf.

As it turned out, the owner of the plant which Rabbi Levy had to inspect was Jewish, and his uncle was the president of the local Jewish community. When he told them of the Rebbe's instructions, they were happy to arrange for him to speak at the *shul*. His delight at the convenient outcome of events turned to dismay, however, as he entered the *shul*. The *shul's* balcony was not used, and the men and the women sat together downstairs without a *mechitzah* to separate between the men's and women's sections of the *shul*.

Rabbi Levy would not join them in their service. After the prayers were concluded, he addressed the congregants and explained to them that a synagogue is G-d's house of prayer and should be designed in the manner which He Himself desires. "My fellow Jews," he concluded, "The Lubavitcher Rebbe has sent a contribution to your *shul*. Why not use it to erect a *mechitzah*."

The community leaders told Rabbi Levy that they were considering constructing a new shul in a different neighborhood. Rabbi Levy convinced them to erect a *mechitzah* and also to build a *mikveh* in the shul. He had the plans for the *mikveh* prepared and sent a Rabbi to supervise the construction.

Some time later, Rabbi Levy received a letter from the Jewish community in the Philippines. "Enclosed," it read, "is a

2.   *Pesachim* 8a.

picture of our new *shul.*" The women's section was attractive and the *mikveh* was both halachically acceptable and architecturally pleasing. "We thought you'd like to know," the letter continued, "that we wrote to the Rebbe before beginning the construction of the new *shul* and the *mikveh,* and his words of encouragement were an inspiration."

This was not the only result of Rabbi Levy's trip. A Jewish student was attending medical school in the Philippines. Although he came from a religious home, he had strayed from Jewish practice and had entered into a relationship with a Philippine woman. He had not attended the synagogue in the Philippines for years, but he was attracted by the news of a lecture from a visiting Rabbi from New York.

The Jewish student waited for Rabbi Levy after the lecture, and they spent an hour talking as they walked back to his hotel. Rabbi Levy could not convince him to give up the Philippine woman immediately, but he maintained contact, and several months later the youth terminated his relationship with the woman.

On another occasion, before a trip to Copenhagen, the Rebbe added a specific directive to his blessings: to check whether the local *mikveh* was halachically acceptable.

As it turned out, Rabbi Levy was able to stay in Copenhagen for only one day, and did not have the opportunity to check the *mikveh.* A year later, before a second trip to Copenhagen, he again sought the Rebbe's blessing for this journey and received exactly the same reply. This time he altered his schedule to make sure that he would be able to check the *mikveh.* With much difficulty, he gained access to the *mikveh* and indeed discovered a *halachic* flaw.

He asked which Rabbinic authority had certified the *mikveh,* and was directed to a leading specialist on *mikvaos,* Rabbi Posen of London.

Rabbi Posen told Rabbi Levy, "I remember the problem with the *mikveh* in Copenhagen. I noticed that flaw and gave them precise instructions how to correct it."

Rabbi Posen promised to deal with the matter promptly. Before concluding their conversation, Rabbi Levy had, however, one more question, "Pardon me for asking, Rabbi Posen. I just wanted to know if you had ever mentioned this matter to the Lubavitcher Rebbe?"

"No," he answered, surprised why Rabbi Levy had thought that he might have done so.

"I could never have undertaken such a responsibility myself," related Rabbi J. J. Hecht. "As soon as I received the information I notified the Rebbe."

What did Rabbi Hecht mean? A few days before Pesach 1987, his son, Rabbi Sholom Ber Hecht of Forest Hills, New York, consulted him about a message that a congregant had received from his nephew.

The nephew and three hundred other Jews had fled from Iran and were temporarily staying in Karachi, Pakistan, where there was no Jewish community. Caught between Iran and Afghanistan, and involved with their own religious disputes with India, the Pakistanis showed no tolerance of other faiths. The man had asked his uncle to send Passover provisions to the refugees, or at least *matzos* for the *Seder* night.

Rabbi Hecht had deep ties with the Iranian community. Thousands of Iranian teenagers had left the country on student visas under his guidance shortly after the Khomeini Revolution. He had made many previous commitments in time, money, and soul. But in this instance, something more was involved; any person spreading Jewish observance in Pakistan was risking his life.

The Rebbe instructed Rabbi Hecht to find somebody who was familiar with Iranian customs and who would agree to travel to Pakistan. The Rebbe added that he would sponsor the trip, purchase the entire amount of *matzos* needed, and offer a blessing to the *shaliach*.

The last particular was more important to Rabbi Hecht than the financial help. It meant that the *shaliach* would be safe.

Soon Rabbi Hecht found a *yeshivah* student, Zalman Gerber, who was willing to undertake the journey. Senator Al D'amato of New York helped him bring the matter to the immediate attention of high-ranking officials in the Pakistani Consulate. However, those officials refused to issue a student visa, clarifying that only those with clear business reasons for journeying to Pakistan could obtain a visa.

This requirement did not dissuade Rabbi Hecht. His associates in the Persian community helped him find a rug dealer, who supplied a letter explaining that Mr. Gerber was journeying to Karachi for two weeks in order to purchase Oriental carpets. The letter worked, and the Pakistanis issued the visa, emphasizing that they could take no responsibility for the traveler's safety.

Arriving in Karachi, Zalman encountered a series of hazards and providential means of overcoming them. The packages of *matzah* which he brought were checked carefully by a customs official, who could not understand what a rug dealer was doing with so many of these strange crackers.

Checking in at the hotel where he had made reservations, he discovered to his dismay that his room was on the eighth floor. Fearful that the hotel staff might grow suspicious after possibly seeing him walk up and down eight flights of stairs on the holiday, he asked to be given a room on a lower floor. Fortunately, this request was allowed, and he moved to an unoccupied second-floor room.

In order to avoid the watchful eyes of Moslem extremists while contacting refugees, the Jews had taken shelter in a deteriorating neighborhood on the outskirts of the city. After they had been located, it was no small feat to transport the boxes of *matzah* without attracting additional attention. Nevertheless, just before commemorating our people's exodus from Egypt, Zalman was able to bring Pesach supplies to this community in the midst of their own journey to freedom.

"Once," relates Rabbi Yitzchak Mishan, the Rabbi of the large Mount Sinai Sephardi community in S. Paulo, Brazil, "a young member of my community asked me to convert his non-Jewish fiancee. I explained that even if the woman would undergo conversion — and I would assist only if she sincerely desired to adopt Judaism, not merely so that she could marry a Jew — he would still be forbidden from marrying her, because he is a *kohen*. The young man was adamant. They had been engaged for five years, and he had no intention of leaving her now.

"I could not convince the man to change his mind. As with other challenges which arise during the course of my activities, I asked for the Rebbe's blessing for success in guiding the young man properly. In matters like this, I don't expect more than a short blessing. I am satisfied with the knowledge that I have brought the issue to the Rebbe's attention.

"To my surprise, shortly after sending this letter, I received a phone call from the office at "770". The Rebbe had given me instructions to continue speaking to the young man. 'You are to explain,' the Rebbe directed, 'that a *kohen* is empowered to bless others — even great people. A person who is not a *kohen* — although he may be a great sage — is not equally empowered. But if, heaven forbid, a *kohen* desecrates his status, he forfeits this great potential.'

"I immediately contacted the young man and invited him for a discussion. I patiently explained the Rebbe's message, but to no avail. The young man had made up his mind and would not budge from his position.

"I could not accept the idea that the Rebbe's answer would be fruitless. Pondering the matter, I read and re-read the Rebbe's words: 'You are to explain...' Perhaps, I thought, this explanation could be addressed to the non-Jewish woman. Maybe this message would have an impact on her...

"I lost no time and invited her to my office. She expressed her deep love for him, stating that she would be willing to undergo whatever is required of her. "I will do anything for this man," she repeated time and again.

"I read aloud from a translated version of the *Kitzur Shulchan Aruch* (the Code of Jewish Law), the prohibition against the marriage of a *kohen* to a convert. I then told her the Rebbe's words, explaining the tremendous loss the man would suffer.

"The woman was moved. 'If he will lose so much because of me, I will not marry him. I love him too much." She was very sincere. Her resolve remained steadfast, and in the next few days, she broke off their relationship.

"Incidentally," Rabbi Mishan concluded, "the young man has since married a fine Jewish woman."

The *shaliach* in Vancouver, Rabbi Yitzchak Wineberg, was considering the most appropriate location to build the *Chabad House*. He asked the Rebbe whether to choose a location near the university, or in the residential area of the city. With his question, he included a map of the city, showing the main areas of population, the shuls, the university, and the main Jewish residential area. The Rebbe underlined the words "residential area" and circled a point on the map in its center, at Oak St. and 41st Ave.

Over the next five years, Rabbi Wineberg looked into purchasing several buildings. Nevertheless, the Rebbe always had reason to reject the acquisitions.

One day, Rabbi Wineberg was informed of a large parking lot that was up for sale. The location seemed attractive, but unfortunately the price was not. The owners were asking half a million dollars for the land. Rabbi Wineberg knew that the subsequent construction would cost even more.

Rabbi Wineberg favored seeking further alternatives. At that time, most other *Chabad* Houses in North America had taken over existing structures, rather than undertake the burden of building their own. And the Rebbe himself had advised Rabbi Wineberg to be conservative when it came to the cost of a building. Once when Rabbi Wineberg had proposed purchasing an existing building that would require a mortgage of $2000 a month, the Rebbe had told him that the people in Vancouver might consider this too great an expense. Nevertheless, he consulted the Rebbe about pursuing the parking lot option and the Rebbe answered in the affirmative.

Together with one of his supporters, a Vancouver businessman named Jack Diamond, Rabbi Wineberg made a trip of several hours to the city of Calgary to visit the company which owned the parking lot. Devout Christians, the owners were impressed by Rabbi Wineberg's cause and reconsidered their offer, lowering the price to $375,000. Rabbi Wineberg told them he would consider the matter and returned to Vancouver.

For Rabbi Wineberg, $375,000 was also a steep price and moreover, the owners wanted the entire sum to be paid immediately. Unsure of how to proceed, he again consulted the Rebbe who gave an encouraging answer. "Continue in this direction. We are now in the month of Adar when we intensify our joy. Plant with joy; sow with joy, build with joy. Success and blessing."

After writing to Calgary to express his interest, but explaining his desire to negotiate regarding the terms, Rabbi Wineberg received a modified proposal from the parking lot owners which certainly must have made him joyous.

The owners agreed to deduct seven thousand dollars from the price. In addition, they asked for a down payment of only $75,000, of which they promised to return $50,000 to the *Chabad* House as a donation, and they agreed to receive the remainder over an extended period of time at a low rate of interest. Moreover, they promised to return the interest as a donation to the *Chabad* House, on the condition that it continue to function as a charitable organization.

The down payment was made with the help of local Lubavitch supporters, plans were quickly prepared for the building, and construction began shortly afterwards. It was completed in the month of Adar, the month of joy, and the first public function in the *Chabad* House was a Purim celebration.

Once, while going through his papers, Rabbi Wineberg happened to notice the original map of the city which he had sent the Rebbe. Until this time, he had assumed that by making a mark, the Rebbe *Shlita* was indicating the general area where the *Chabad* House should be located. Now, standing in the building of the *Chabad* House, he saw that it had been constructed on the precise point of the map which the Rebbe had marked.

"As our activities expanded," Rabbi Wineberg concluded, "we realized that we could not have hoped for a more central and convenient location."

≋

Rabbi Yonah Fradkin of San Diego, California, had not deliberately set out to challenge the calendar. But the final decision to establish a local day school was made three weeks before the opening of the school year. As he worked around the clock to raise funds and enroll students, he was told about a seemingly insurmountable hurdle: "It will take at least three months before you can obtain a building permit."

At that point, he consulted with the Rebbe. "May your efforts be crowned with abundant success," replied the Rebbe in blessing. Encouraged, Rabbi Fradkin labored strenuously to reach his goal. As he continued, he indeed found success in every dimension of the undertaking. Funds were raised, a site was located, and students were enrolled, but that one hurdle seemed to be indeed insurmountable.

"It's simply unrealistic to expect the permit to materialize so quickly," he was told. "There are hundreds of buildings waiting for inspection before their permits are issued. Your application has no chance of receiving priority over all the others."

One evening, there was a knock on the Fradkin door. "Hello. I am the city hall representative in charge of granting building permits. May I have a chat with you?" asked the gentleman at the door.

The man told Rabbi Fradkin that he was experiencing a very trying family problem. "I am in need of Divine assistance and I am eager to do a good deed so that I may merit it. Yesterday, someone told me that the Lubavitcher Rebbe's *shaliach* in the city is trying to build a school and has applied for a building permit. I would like to help."

"At the very beginning of our *shlichus* in Vienna, Austria," relates Rabbi Yaakov Yitzchak Biederman, "we reported to the Rebbe about our first activities in the city. The Rebbe responded favorably and wished us success in our efforts. At the end of his letter he added, 'specifically in the sacred work of education, in kindergartens.'

"We were greatly encouraged by the Rebbe's blessings and the regard he showed for our work by adding a handwritten message. However, we had no kindergarten.

"Several days later, we were approached by some parents. 'We know you are new in our city,' they said, 'but we've heard about the worldwide Lubavitch educational network. Here in Vienna, many Jewish children are not receiving any Jewish education at all. Perhaps you would consider opening a kindergarten?'"

When Rabbi Avrohom Yitzchok Glick from London, the future initiator of a Lubavitch presence in many countries in Europe, entered the Rebbe's study for *yechidus* in the early 'seventies, the Rebbe asked what business he was in.

Rabbi Glick replied that he manufactured light bulbs and traveled throughout Europe to sell his products and to purchase raw materials. He had recently traveled to Malaga in Southern Spain for supplies.

"A person in the lighting business," the Rebbe replied, "knows that a bulb must be lit. Every Jew is like a light bulb, and we should help him glow. When you return to Malaga, please add to your agenda an inquiry about the spiritual needs of the Jews living there."

During a later *yechidus*, the Rebbe asked Rabbi Glick if there was a *mikveh* in Malaga. Despite his doubts about how much use this *mikveh* would receive, Rabbi Glick resolved to have a kosher *mikveh* constructed there.

On his next trip to Spain, Rabbi Glick heard about a Jewish businessman who was interested in building a strictly *kosher* hotel in Malaga and who was seeking a Rabbinic authority to guide him through the project. Rabbi Glick realized the opportunity and asked the Rebbe whether to pursue the matter. "Go immediately, even today," replied the Rebbe.

The businessman was happy to meet Rabbi Glick, who explained that the hotel would have to employ a resident *mashgiach* who would supervise the *kashrus* of the food prepared at the hotel. "Obviously," continued Rabbi Glick, "the relocation of a *mashgiach* and his family to Malaga means that you would have to construct a kosher *mikveh*."

The businessman readily agreed to Rabbi Glick's condition, and Rabbi Glick agreed to find a Lubavitch family who would couple the supervision of the hotel's kitchen with *shlichus*. This initiated Lubavitch activity in Spain, and represented a significant step in the Jewish return to that country, half a millennium after the Expulsion of 1492.

Chapter 4 —
Encouraging Jewish Advancement

Dr. David Weiss has achieved world renown for his work in cancer research. Although he came from an observant home, his involvement in American culture presented him with many challenges. His encounters with the chassidim and the philosophy of Lubavitch helped him overcome these hurdles.

Once while at *yechidus* with the Rebbe, he asked him if he could consider himself a chassid. "I am attracted to the chassidic way of life," he explained, "but can never see myself donning a black hat or chassidic garb. Does this disqualify me?"

The Rebbe responded, "When a Jew endeavors to take a step forward in the service of G-d and the love of his fellow man every day, I am happy to consider him my chassid." This is the thrust of this chapter: to share examples of how the Rebbe has personally encouraged people to advance in Jewish practice.

"I was one of the counselors who led *Shabbos* parties for Jewish children during the period before the Rebbe assumed leadership of the chassidic movement," relates Rabbi Moshe Lasker. "Each week, I would submit a report of the activities to "770".

"One Friday, as I submitted my report at "770", the Rebbe called me to his office. 'Are you busy?' he asked.

"I realized that he wanted to delegate a responsibility to me, so I immediately answered that I was not. The Rebbe then told me: 'Please take two candles and visit this Jewish woman in the hospital. Ask her to light them. If the hospital staff protests about the regulations, try to work it out. If the woman herself is hesitant, tell her that Rabbi Schneerson requested that she light *Shabbos* candles.'

"I hurried towards the subway to carry out my mission. I met the woman and gave her the message. She was indeed reluctant at first, but when I mentioned that the Rebbe had sent me, she readily agreed. I enlisted the cooperation of the non-Jewish nurse who promised to assist her and to move the candles to a safe place.

"I rushed home, arriving just ten minutes before *Shabbos*. Seconds after I walked through the door, the telephone rang. 'This is Schneerson speaking,' the voice on the line said. 'Has Moshe arrived home yet?'

"A few weeks later, while I was in "770", I felt a friendly tap on my shoulder from the Rebbe. "*Yasher Koach* for fulfilling the mission," he told me.

A young Lubavitch *yeshivah* student quickened his step down one of Manhattan's busy boulevards. It was Friday afternoon, and he still had some more rounds to make. He was on his way to one of his 'regulars' — a businessman whom he visited every Friday, sharing the messages of the Rebbe's *mitzvah* campaigns.

As he entered the store, he noticed a marked change in the interior.

"Don't ask!" the businessman greeted him with a strained look on his face. "My place has been flooded. I lost a great deal of merchandise. I've written a letter to the Rebbe requesting a blessing for a successful turn of fortune. Would you please deliver it for me?"

The *yeshivah* student assured the businessman that he would do so. As soon as an answer came, he hurried to notify his friend in Manhattan. "The Rebbe has instructed you to be meticulous in keeping *Shabbos* and *Yom-Tov* (festivals)" he told him.

The businessman was visibly agitated. "What does that mean?" he retorted indignantly. "I do observe *Shabbos* and the holidays."

The student decided to inform the Rebbe of the man's response. The Rebbe answered tersely: "The **onset** of *Shabbos* and *Yom-Tov.*"

That Friday, the student brought news of the Rebbe's second answer to the businessman. Trying to help him put the Rebbe's directive into practice, he inquired about the man's routine on Friday nights.

"Well, obviously, I say *Kiddush* and sit down to a *Shabbos* meal."

Suddenly, a thought came to the student's mind. "When do you close your business on Fridays?" he asked.

"Oh, about seven or eight," the man replied naively. During the ensuing conversation, the businessman learned for the first time about the correct time for the onset of *Shabbos* and holidays.

"I had studied in a *yeshivah* for many years, but had not been exposed to *Chassidus*," related a young man in *Eretz Yisrael.* "As I began to question my purpose in life and to search for deeper meaning, I met some Lubavitcher chassidim, and was very impressed by the depth, meaning, and joy of their way of life. I began to study *Chassidus* and spend more time within the chassidic community.

"Although I felt a strong attraction, many elements of the chassidic way of life differed from those of my family and of my *yeshivah.* I decided to ask the Rebbe about my concerns and apprehensions.

"A few weeks later, the Rebbe sent me a detailed answer to all of my questions. I felt satisfied and no longer hesitated about my involvement with *Chassidus.* The Rebbe also added a puzzling postscript: 'There is no need to ask why *Chassidus* was not revealed in previous generations,' and proceeded to explain this concept in full.[1] This issue had not bothered me at all, and I had mentioned nothing to this effect in my letter.

"Soon my interest in *Chassidus* became known in my *yeshivah.* One day, a Torah scholar whom I admired and respected asked me to have a talk with him. I knew that he wanted to discourage me from the new path which I had begun to explore.

"He presented many arguments against the study of *Chassidus,* and I countered all of them successfully. I realized that his objections stemmed from his lack of familiarity with the subject.

"He then unsheathed what he thought would be his most convincing argument. 'If *Chassidus* is so valuable, then why,' he asked, 'was its study not revealed to previous generations?'

---

1.   The subject is discussed in *Likkutei Sichos,* Vol. XXX, p. 171ff. See sources cited there in footnote 22.

"He was surprised at both the speed and the depth with which I answered his question."

One of the unique dimensions of *yechidus*, a private meeting with the Rebbe, is the Rebbe's ability to find an answer which satisfies the person asking the question. For example, although he had maintained an interest in *Chabad* activities for an extended time, one of the young men in contact with Rabbi Berl Shemtov, the *shaliach* in Detroit, would not agree to put on *tefillin*. "I am a thorough person," he explained, "and I don't feel ready to make a commitment which must be fulfilled every day without any possibility for a break."

Rabbi Shemtov convinced him to visit the Rebbe for a *yechidus*. When he emerged from the Rebbe's study, he told his friends that he had decided to put on *tefillin* every day. "But what about your hesitation to commit yourself on a daily basis?"

"The Rebbe resolved that for me," said the young man with a smile. "He told me that there was always one day a week — *Shabbos* — when I would not be required to perform this *mitzvah*."

Eliezer Steinman was a well-known Israeli authority on Chassidism. He wrote about various chassidic streams, including Lubavitch. Before writing about Lubavitch, Mr. Steinman contacted the chassidic writer, Rabbi Chanoch Glitzenstein of Jerusalem, for source material. Being an author himself, Rabbi Glitzenstein wondered whether a person who did not live a chassidic lifestyle would be able to communicate an authentic picture.

He consulted the Rebbe, who encouraged him to assist Mr. Steinman, despite his secular orientation. The Rebbe added that Rabbi Glitzenstein should refrain from making any comments about religious practice.

Rabbi Glitzenstein offered Mr. Steinman extensive help and direction. Although as a Lubavitch chassid committed to outreach, it was difficult to avoid any mention of religious practice, he was careful to follow the Rebbe's directive. In time, Mr. Steinman himself initiated a direct contact with the Rebbe and began to correspond with him.

Over the many months of contact with Rabbi Glitzenstein, the author and his wife began to seek his assistance in obtaining various religious items. Beginning with a request for a *machzor* from which they could pray during the High Holidays, the couple soon inquired about other religious necessities. At their own pace, the Steinmans made a turnover in their lifestyle, creating quite a sensation in the cultural circles of secular Israeli society.

Some time later, Mr. Steinman confided in Rabbi Glitzenstein. "You should know that throughout our relationship, I was expecting you to lecture me on religion. I had planned to reproach you for foisting your beliefs on others. But contrary to my expectations, you respected my tendency to make my own decisions, and did not mention my personal religious practice at all. That was more convincing to me than any lecture."

"This incident occurred in the early years of the Rebbe's leadership," relates Rabbi Sholom Ber Gordon. "I became friendly with a family in Newark, New Jersey, where I was serving as a *shaliach*. The parents were anxious to see their older daughter happily married and settled, but she remained single.

"After becoming better acquainted, I told them about the power of the Rebbe's blessings. 'I come from the Ukraine,' the mother told me. 'I am familiar with Rebbeim and have sought their counsel in the past. I would actually like to visit this Rebbe of yours and receive a blessing for my daughter.'

"I arranged for a *yechidus* and traveled with the mother and an older son to Brooklyn. I waited for them outside while they entered the Rebbe's study. We met after the *yechidus* and the woman was very upset. 'What happened?' I asked.

"'The Rebbe inquired about our source of income,' she explained, 'I told him that although we were financially secure and could easily retire, we still maintain our business for the sake of our unmarried daughter. We are concerned about her welfare and want to provide for her future.

"The Rebbe asked about *Shabbos* and I replied that the business was open on *Shabbos*.

"'Why?' inquired the Rebbe. 'You've described your family's income as financially secure. Why then do you work on *Shabbos?*'

"'I explained to the Rebbe that it was not for our sake that we kept the business open on *Shabbos*, but for our daughter's future. I then requested the Rebbe's blessing for a good match. I promised that as soon as she would marry and settle down, we would close the business on *Shabbos*.

"'G-d wants it to be the other way around,' the Rebbe replied. 'First close the business on *Shabbos*. I assure you that afterwards your daughter will find a suitable match.'

"The mother concluded indignantly, 'Back in Ukraine, I would often consult Rebbeim. They always offered their blessings, and they never asked about our Torah conduct.'

"Mother and son returned to Newark and resumed their daily routine. Over ten years elapsed since that *yechidus*. The father passed away, the business remained open on *Shabbos*, and the daughter remained single.

"In the mid-sixties, sporadic demonstrations and riots erupted in cities throughout the country. Soon enough, the streets of Newark were also rampaged and violent mobs burned and looted many places of work. This family's business was among those which were ruined. At her advanced age, and after such an experience, the mother did not consider opening it again. Thus it remained closed the entire week, including *Shabbos*.

"A few months later, the daughter was introduced to a very nice, observant and learned man who also came from a wealthy family. Later I was invited to officiate at the wedding. Incidentally, although the bride was over forty at the time, the couple did have a child, who grew up to be a Torah scholar in Eretz Yisrael."

In the first years of the Rebbe's leadership, during the *far-brengen* of Purim 1953, the Rebbe told one of the participants to study *Chassidus*. The person voiced his hesitation; he had never been trained in this system of thought, nor did he understand how this study would contribute to his personal development.

The Rebbe replied with a rhetorical question: "When you board a train, do you fully comprehend its precise mechanical functioning?

"When a passenger sits in the coach, whether he understands how it works or not — the train crew will perform their task, and the train will transport its travelers to their desired destinations."

Yaakov, a taxi owner from Tel Aviv, was accustomed to driving others. Now, however, it was his creditors who were driving him — to desperation.

He thought the purchase of his own cab would increase his income, because it would save him from paying a monthly percentage for a company taxi. Instead, the purchase plunged him deeper into debt. He exhausted the resources that friends and family could give him, and the interest on bank loans was devouring a major source of his income. Furthermore, he was beginning to discover that it was costly to maintain his own taxi.

Yaakov needed an urgent thousand-dollar loan, but to whom could he turn? Finally, he thought of asking the other drivers in his company. It was embarrassing — they were not well-off themselves, but he had no other alternative; he needed money urgently.

He thought of Amnon, a decent, *shomer-Shabbos* taxi driver. Amnon was often taunted by the other drivers. "Ridiculous! Most of our income comes from *Shabbos* fares when there is limited bus service." They mocked Amnon's parked taxi. "Lease it to someone else over *Shabbos*, Amnon. At least make some commission."

Amnon refused. "No one is going to desecrate the *Shabbos* with my taxi!" he replied with quiet determination.

Yaakov was surprised when Amnon offered to lend him the entire sum. He hadn't expected him to agree so readily, and he certainly did not think that he would have had such a sum available. He had hoped for no more than part of the amount and for advice on whom to approach for the balance of the money.

But Amnon added, "Before I give you the money, I want you to hear me out," Amnon said.

Though he was in no mood for conversation, Yaakov had no choice but to listen. "Listen," began Amnon. "I experienced the same hassle you are going through when I first started out. I worked day and night, and I still couldn't get out of debt."

"Yes," Yaakov mumbled. "I remember."

Amnon continued, "You might also remember that my son became critically ill. My wife and I struggled during the weeks he was in and out of the hospital, but the doctors could not cure him. We even tried different kinds of natural remedies and healing charms, but nothing helped. One day, an observant neighbor with whom I had little contact stopped me in the hallway.

"Do you mind if I have a word with you?' he asked politely. 'I would like to give you some advice concerning your sick son.'

"I was inclined to shrug him off, but I was so emotionally spent that I listened wearily. 'A Rabbi in New York has helped many people in time of need,' he said. 'Let me give you his address. You have nothing to lose by requesting his blessing.'

"The name and address he gave me was that of Rabbi M. M. Schneerson at "770" Eastern Parkway. In reply to my letter, Rabbi Schneerson gave my son a blessing and directed me to incorporate *Shabbos*, *kashrus*, and *tefillin* into my life. It was a difficult transition, but let me tell you, my son recovered. And since we started keeping *Shabbos*, my income has been steady and sufficient. We have even managed to save some money."

Amnon took a deep breath. "The money that I will lend you comes from keeping *Shabbos*. I'd like you to try to keep *Shabbos* for a while as part of our loan agreement."

Yaakov needed the money and agreed to start observing *Shabbos*. As a result, many things in his life changed for the better. Within several months, he repaid the loan.

Yaakov was not the last person in the chain of *Shabbos* adherents which began with the Rebbe's directive to Amnon.

✎

Chapter 5 —
With Sensitivity, Purpose, and Vitality

It is related that the Maggid of Mezritch once
looked at an earthenware vessel and then told his
disciples that it had been made by a man who was
blind in his left eye. The disciples checked and
verified that indeed the potter was only able to see
with his right eye.

Were the Maggid's statements an expression of
ruach hakodesh (Divinely-inspired intuition)?

No. As the Maggid pointed out, the shape of the
vessel testified to the characteristics of the person
who fashioned it. Still none of the disciples were
able to make such a distinction. Apparently, the
Maggid's *ruach hakodesh* had sensitized his ordinary
powers of perception, making it possible for them to
ascertain distinctions to which most ordinary people
would be oblivious.

Similar concepts apply with regard to the unique
dimensions of the Rebbe's personality. As reflected in
many of the stories in this book, the Rebbe's conduct
shows spiritual qualities which most men have not
developed. But at least as significant are those
stories which show how the Rebbe's spiritual
attainments have shaped those dimensions of his

character which are shared by others and which enable him to reflect a unique measure of sensitivity, purpose, and energy.

A young Russian immigrant who had migrated to in America in 1955, entangled himself unknowingly with the law. Unfamiliar with postal regulations, he violated several postal rules and was subpoenaed to appear in court. The immigrant wrote the Rebbe of his predicament and requested his counsel. The Rebbe advised him on the issue, then added:

"Integrity in such matters is well known among Lubavitcher chassidim. When the *Tzemach Tzedek* would send a letter by messenger, he would simultaneously compensate the postal authority for the loss in postal charges, paying the appropriate postage to the local post-office. His chassidim have always aspired to emulate his example."

⚭

At a chassidic *farbrengen*, Rabbi Leibel Groner, the Rebbe's private secretary, once told the following story: After receiving an assignment from the Rebbe, one chassid felt overwhelmed; what the Rebbe was asking of him seemed to be beyond his capabilities.

The Rebbe noticed his hesitation and remarked softly: "My expectations of myself are ten times beyond my capacity."

⚭

In a similar vein, Rabbi David Hollander tells of a brief encounter with the Rebbe when he came to receive the *lekach* (honey cake) which the Rebbe customarily distributes on *Erev Yom Kippur*.

"May you be blessed with success both as a Rabbi and as a private citizen," the Rebbe told him.

"I had been contemplating leaving the rabbinate," related Rabbi Hollander, who had devoted scores of tireless and active years to public service. "And so, when the Rebbe mentioned 'private citizen', I immediately informed him of my thoughts."

"Heaven forbid!' the Rebbe replied. 'Look at me, I am constantly undertaking additional responsibilities. What room is there to consider a leave or vacation?'"

Once, the chassidim indeed suggested to the Rebbe that he take a brief respite from his non-stop schedule and go away for a short vacation. As a spokesman, they chose the elder chassid, Reb Nissan Nemanov. Reb Nissan summoned up all of his powers of persuasion, but to no avail. He tried to explain that all the previous Rebbeim had gone on vacation from time to time. "Why," he concluded, "shouldn't the Rebbe do so as well?"

The Rebbe smiled and replied, "When the chassidim sat and studied, the Rebbeim could go on vacation. Today, it's the chassidim who go on vacation, so the Rebbe must stay and study."

The Rebbe constantly encourages the publishing of sacred Jewish texts, particularly those of previous Lubavitcher Rebbeim. And with a revolutionary thrust in the Torah world, he has urged the compilation of detailed indexes for the numerous texts published.

In the winter of 1980, the Rebbe requested that a comprehensive index be compiled for all the texts authored by the founder of Lubavitch-*Chabad*, Rabbi Shneur Zalman of Liadi. The challenge of preparing the index was increased by the Rebbe's deadline: the project was to be completed within two weeks so that it could be published for the upcoming chassidic holiday of *Yud-Tes Kislev*, the anniversary of Rabbi Shneur Zalman's release from a Czarist prison.

"We worked around the clock," recalls Rabbi Menashe Perman, who was involved in the project. "In addition to our desire to meet the Rebbe's deadline, we were continuously inspired by the fact that the Rebbe himself edited the material meticulously every day, verifying every entry, and making additions and corrections.

"When the work was completed, the Rebbe instructed us to include in the book a list of the people who had worked on the project. We compiled a list and handed it in to the Rebbe, who casually added his own name.

"When type-setting this page, we placed the Rebbe's name at the top of the page. However, the Rebbe insisted that his name be included in alphabetical order, together with the others. The list of contributing editors to this index is arranged according to first names. In the middle of all the others, you can find a familiar name which begins with the Hebrew letter *Mem.*"

When the Rebbe was a child, before his father was appointed *rav* in Yekatrinoslav, his family lived in Nikolayev. Once a pogrom once broke out. Fearful of the danger, the Jews concealed themselves until the peril passed. His mother took him and his brothers to a shelter, where they joined many other women and children.

Some of the terrified children began to cry loudly. This was very dangerous, because their cries could lead the violent rioters to their hiding place. While everyone else was paralyzed with fright, the Rebbe who was less than five at the time, calmly soothed the crying children one by one with a pat on the cheek, a finger to the mouth, and so forth, until quiet was restored.

The Rebbe's family once spent a summer in Balaclava, by the shore of the Black Sea in Crimea. One day, the vacationers heard that a young boy had gone out alone in a small boat. The boat had capsized far from shore, and the child faced imminent danger.

Another boy swam out to the boat and rescued the drowning child. Hurrying to the scene of the incident, the Rebbe's mother discovered that the "hero" was none other than her nine-year-old son.

The Rebbe's father was Rabbi of the city and his house was a constant hub of activity, but the Rebbe usually did not allow this to disrupt his schedule. He stayed in his room, absorbed in the study of the Torah.

One of the few times that he became involved in public affairs was at the age of twenty, when a typhus epidemic caused many deaths in the city. He worked day and night to aid the victims and to recruit others to help.

As a result, he contracted the dread disease himself. His body burned with fever, and his lips moved incessantly. In his delirium, he spoke about the spiritual realms of *Atzilus* and *Asiyah* and the positive virtue generated in these spheres by Jewish devotion in the physical world.

Rabbi Yochanan Gordon served as *gabbai* of the *shul* in "770", and was manager of a *gemach* (free loan fund) which was established in the days of the Previous Rebbe, the *Rayatz*. Every year, Rabbi Gordon presented a financial report of the *gemach's* income and expenses.[1]

---

1.   Rabbi Gordon would submit his report prior to the *Shabbos* when we read the Torah portion of *Mishpatim* which includes the verse *(Exodus 22:24)*: "And when you will lend money...."

In the winter of 1950, several weeks after the Previous Rebbe passed away, Rabbi Gordon presented the report to the Rebbe *Shlita*.

Rabbi Gordon was surprised at the Rebbe's response to his report: "Can this be considered a *gemach* prepared to meet the needs of the Jewish community in New York?"

"We have a Rebbe with a broad vision who will demand much from us," Rabbi Gordon told his fellow chassidim. And indeed, the Rebbe continued to make demands of Rabbi Gordon and the *gemach*. For example, years later, in response to one of Rabbi Gordon's annual reports, the Rebbe asked why a *gemach* that was created to lend money had so much cash in reserve.

Together with millions of others, the Rebbe and his wife Rebbetzin Chaya Mushka ע"ה were uprooted from their home during World War II. Shortly after the Nazis rose to power, the Rebbe and the Rebbetzin moved from Berlin, where they had been living for several years, to Paris. They fled Paris in mid-1940 on one of the last trains before the German invasion, and arrived at Vichy, which served as a haven for fleeing Jews.

Vichy was under Italian rule, and the Italians were less Anti-Semitic than their German allies. Nevertheless, it was only relatively safe; life in any location in a Nazi Europe was dangerous and insecure for Jews.

The local hotels did not open their doors willingly to the helpless refugees. In order to enter a hotel, a guest had to prove that he possessed at least one hundred dollars. This was obviously way beyond the meager means of most refugees.

The Rebbe had a single one hundred dollar bill. He ventured out to the streets seeking needy refugees. Handing over the bill, he directed the refugee to the hotel at which he was staying. After the refugee was admitted, he slipped the bill back to the Rebbe unnoticed. The Rebbe returned to the streets with the 'door-opening' bill, seeking another 'customer.'

Among the many difficult regulations placed upon the citizens of a country at war was the demand to sell all privately-owned gold to the government. One day, a desperate Jew knocked on the Rebbe's door. "Please help me. Selling my gold at tremendous loss would totally ruin me and crush my family's ability to survive this terrible war. Please hide my gold in your apartment." The Rebbe readily agreed to help a fellow Jew. The golden nuggets were hidden in a closet in the tiny apartment.

Soon afterwards, the Italians began searching the refugees' dwellings for gold. The Rebbetzin ע"נ worried that holding the man's fortune might endanger their own lives, for illegal possession of gold was a capital offense. "Perhaps we should transfer the gold elsewhere," she suggested anxiously. The Rebbe was adamant. "No. A fellow-Jew entrusted us with his entire fortune, and it is our duty to protect it."

Meantime, desperate efforts were being made across the ocean by the Previous Rebbe, Rabbi Yosef Yitzchak Schneersohn, to facilitate the immigration of the Rebbe and the Rebbetzin to America.

After endless and urgent telephone calls, telegrams, and hours of effort, the necessary papers and boat tickets were obtained for the couple. They were scheduled to embark from Portugal and made the trip there uneventfully. Shortly before boarding the ship to America, the Rebbe received a telegram from his father-in-law. "Do not journey on this ship," was the short and astounding message.

Without as much as a blink of an eye, the Rebbe canceled the reservations and waited for the next departure. Later, it was discovered that the first ship had been sunk by German U-boats. There were no survivors. The Rebbe and the Rebbetzin, by contrast, arrived safely in New York on the 28th of Sivan, 5701 (1941).

"In my eyes, the most amazing aspect of this incident," says one chassid, "is not the farsightedness of the Previous Rebbe, but the Rebbe's unquestioning acceptance of the Previous Rebbe's directive. He obtained the required papers and tickets by a series of miracles. The Nazis were aware of their identity, and there was no certainty of an additional departure. Any delay could have jeopardized their possibility for escape. Yet, as their lives hung in balance, the Rebbe followed his father-in-law's directive without a second thought."

During the early morning hours on Simchas Torah, an elderly chassid walked over to a group of young men who had taken a brief recess from the continuous dancing in "770".

"Tired, eh?" he commented with a smile. There was no need for an answer; their red faces, limp hands, and drenched clothes said it all.

"Let me tell about one Simchas Torah night in the late 1940s right here in "770", while the Previous Rebbe was alive. The Rebbe *Shlita* — we used to call him by his initials, 'the *RaMaSh*' — was dancing all night, from 10 p.m. till 7 a.m., as he always did on Simchas Torah. None of us, not even the most energetic, could keep up with him.

"At one point, one of the Previous Rebbe's household attendants came down to the *shul*. Although the Previous Rebbe's quarters were on the third floor of "770", he was worried that the noise of the singing and dancing might disturb the Previous Rebbe's rest.

"Someone approached the Rebbe *Shlita* and whispered the attendant's message into his ear. In response, the Rebbe removed his shoes, and continued to dance barefoot all night long, singing a melody softly and saying, 'Sha...sha...sha,' instead of the words."

～～

"The flight to *Eretz Yisrael* took many hours," reminisced Rabbi Shimon Goldman. "I needed to get up and stretch my legs. As I walked down the aisle, a fellow passenger, who was obviously an observant Jew, stopped me. 'Excuse me, sir,' he said. 'You look familiar. Have we met before?'

"'Have you ever lived in Crown Heights,' I asked curiously.

"'No,' my companion replied.

"'Do you have business dealings in South Africa?' I enquired. 'My son runs the Chabad House there.' Again, my companion demurred.

"'Do you live in Flatbush, New York?' I continued. 'I have a store in that neighborhood.'

"'No, I live in Queens.' He pondered for a moment, and then a thought entered his mind. 'Perhaps you are a Lubavitcher?' he inquired.

"'Yes.'

"'Are you involved with Lubavitch institutions?'

"It did not take long to put the pieces together. I had participated in a board meeting in an effort to facilitate government funding for *Beis Rivkah*, the Lubavitch school for girls. My companion had attended the same meeting, as a consultant.

"'I have a story to tell you,' the man continued. 'I am the vice-president of a well-known college. Although my schedule is very demanding, I try my best to devote some time to Jewish education. I have used my experience with the local bureaucracy to assist Jewish institutions by preparing the necessary applications for state and federal funding. Although this process is long, tedious, and demands much effort, I consider it my contribution to the future of Torah study.

"I have, thank G-d, met with success. I received much satisfaction from seeing schools and institutions awarded necessary funding. In recent months, however, I noticed a marked change in governmental response to the applications I presented. My long hours of paperwork went unrewarded, as one application after another was turned down. I decided to investigate the reason.

"After a meticulous follow-through, I discovered that the applications had not even reached the federal offices. They were aborted at the state level by a Jewish clerk who deliberately sought petty flaws in every application.

"I felt personally slighted and distressed. Not only had many hours of labor been unproductive, but more significantly, the schools had not received the funding.

"I often drive into Brooklyn to see the Rebbe when he distributes charity on Sundays. One Sunday afternoon, I arrived in Crown Heights, feeling very upset about the applications that I had worked on.

"When my turn in line came, I briefly described the situation to the Rebbe. I was so agitated about the matter that I blurted out: 'In the past, when a person stood in the way of benefiting the Jewish people, our leaders would make sure that they could interfere no longer. This is what I am asking regarding that Jewish clerk....'

"The Rebbe listened patiently and then responded: 'Even if one considers another person to be ninety percent lacking in goodness and merit, one must nevertheless remember that he still maintains ten percent of positive virtue.'"

An entry in a *yeshivah* student's diary from 1952: "The Rebbe *Shlita* has instructed *yeshivah* students to visit *shuls* in

Crown Heights and the surrounding neighborhoods every *Shabbos* and to share chassidic discourses with the congregants.

"I and the other participating students prepared a weekly report of the *shul* visits. The Rebbe was pleased with the report, but not completely satisfied. The bottom of the report had the following response: 'Next week's report should be twice as long.'"

Chapter 6 —
To Be a Rebbe

A group of chassidim once came to R. Yisrael of Ruzhin, complaining of a drought that was jeopardizing their crops and their livestock. R. Yisrael led them through shaded paths in the nearby forest until he came upon a particular tree. He motioned to the chassidim to sit and said:

"When there was a drought in the time of the Baal Shem Tov, he would bring his chassidim to this tree, sing a melody, share a teaching, and rain would come.

"A generation later, when there was a drought, my grandfather the Maggid of Mezritch would also bring his followers to this tree. He would tell them this story of the Baal Shem Tov and say, 'Although I no longer remember the teaching, this is the melody the Baal Shem would sing.' And after he sang the melody, rain came down.

"As for me," R. Yisrael concluded, "I know neither the melody nor the teaching. But I do know the story. May relating the story bring rain."

Reb Yisrael and his chassidim had barely
emerged from the forest before the first
thunderbursts were heard.

*   *   *

Many of the stories in this book show the
contemporary dimension of the Rebbe's leadership,
how he is involved with people and situations which
the Rebbeim of previous generations did not
encounter. But it cannot be forgotten, that he is the
heir to the tradition of those previous Rebbeim; that
he perpetuates the uniqueness of the Rebbe-chassid
relationship that existed in previous generations.
This is the focus of the present chapter.

One cloudy night during the first years after the Rebbe assumed his position, a group of people stood outside of "770" for *Kiddush Levanah*, the sanctification of the moon. These prayers may be recited only when it is possible to see the moon clearly during the first half of the Jewish month.[1]

And on this wintry night in Brooklyn, it was the fourteenth night of the month and the Rebbe and a group of his chassidim were watching a cloud-covered sky. As they were waiting, the Rebbe began telling a story about a similar situation which occurred with a Rebbe and his European chassidim almost two hundred years before.

Reb Meir of Premishlan and his followers, the Rebbe related, had faced a similar situation. It was the last night in which the moon could be sanctified, but it was covered with clouds. Reb Meir turned to his followers. "How did the Jews recite *Kiddush Levanah* prayers in the desert?" he asked. "Their camp was covered by the Clouds of Glory."

His followers sensed that his question was rhetorical and remained silent.

Reb Meir soon continued. "Moshe Rabbeinu took a handkerchief, waved it at the position in the sky where the moon would be located, and the clouds parted." And Reb Meir took out his own handkerchief, waved it at the clouds, and they too moved apart, revealing the full moon.

"Perhaps it can happen again," the Rebbe asked his own followers. "Can somebody here can do the same thing?"

While the others remained silent, one elder chassid boldly suggested that the Rebbe do it.

The Rebbe quietly went inside to his office. Seconds later, the clouds parted to reveal the bright moon. As the Rebbe emerged to recite the prayers, the chassidim whispered to

---

1. More particularly, it is customary to sanctify the moon from the seventh night of the month onward.

each other that the Rebbe must have waved a handkerchief at the clouds from the solitude of his room.

The story continues forty years later, and thousands of miles away, in the beautiful southern British sea resort of Bournemouth. The Rebbe *Shlita* had announced a campaign to spread the practice of *Kiddush Levanah*,[2] so the town's *shluchim*, Rabbi and Mrs. Alperovitz, decided to introduce this ritual by performing it during a late-night boat cruise.

At first, interest in the cruise was small and Rabbi Alperovitz thought of canceling the event. As they prepared to do so, they received a message of encouragement from the Rebbe *Shlita*. With dedication and enthusiasm, they increased their efforts. On the night the cruise was scheduled, forty people came to the harbor, despite forecasts of heavy clouds and thunderstorms.

The program was impressive and the storms held back, but the sky remained covered with clouds and the *Kiddush Levanah* prayers could not be recited. As the boat was about to head back to the pier, Rabbi Alperovitz told the handkerchief story, and everyone looked heavenward expectantly. Someone must have waved a handkerchief, because the clouds began to part, revealing a beautiful, clear moon.

Rabbi Yehudah Liebush Heber and his family were very close to the Rebbe and the Rebbetzin during World War II, when the couple lived anonymously in Paris.

"At the beginning of the war," related Rabbi Heber, "I was deliberating whether to stay in Paris or to try to immigrate to the States. This was before the Nazi invasion of Paris, and no one could predict how devastating the future would be. I was

---

2.   See the essay entitled "The Sanctification of the Moon," in *Sound the Great Shofar* (Kehot, N.Y., 1992), p. 97.

financially secure in Paris and concerned about the uncertainty and difficulty of immigration."

The Rebbe suggested that I consult with his father-in-law, the Previous Rebbe, who was living in Poland.

"I was very surprised by this advice. Contact with Warsaw was virtually impossible by phone or mail. "Send a telegram," the Rebbe suggested. This also seemed futile, because telegrams were not being delivered either.

"'You have no idea,' the Rebbe said, 'what a Rebbe is. The letter and the telegram need not be delivered in order for the Rebbe to know the question. And the Rebbe's response need not arrive in order for you to receive your answer.'

"I promptly sat down to phrase my question and proceeded to the Western Union office. 'Sorry, there is absolutely no possibility of telegraphing Poland,' said the clerk. 'All the lines are down.' I did not really expect otherwise, but I had done what I could.

"The next morning I awoke with a sudden clarity. Despite my previous hesitations, I suddenly felt very adamant about leaving Paris and immigrating to the States."

Rabbi Heber arrived in the States in 1940, a few months before the Rebbe. His family maintained a close relationship with the Rebbe and the Rebbetzin for many years to follow.

The Rebbe was conducting his Pesach *seder*. When it was time to eat the *afikoman*, the Rebbe inquired about a group of *yeshivah* students who had been sent to serve as *shluchim* to promote the growth of the Lubavitch Yeshivah in Melbourne, Australia. The students had returned to New York for the holiday.

The Rebbe was informed that the young men were staying at "770", and they were quickly summoned. The Rebbe handed each of the *shluchim* a piece of the *afikoman.* "It is written," the Rebbe said, "that one must give each member of his household a piece of the *afikoman.* The *shluchim* are members of my household. In truth, all the *yeshivah* students are my children. Still, the *shluchim* command special attention."

Although today's generation has grown accustomed to overseas travel, it was much less convenient and affordable during the first years of the Rebbe's leadership. Nevertheless, one of the *shluchim* from Europe arranged a trip to "770" in order to celebrate *Yud-Beis Tammuz,* the anniversary of the Previous Rebbe's release from prison, and to participate in the Rebbe's *farbrengen.*

Yud-Beis Tammuz comes out during the summer camping season. Shortly before the *farbrengen,* the *shaliach* was contacted by the staff of the Lubavitch camp in upstate New York. "Please spend the night of *Yud-Beis Tammuz* with our campers," he was asked. "We have not been able to find anyone else who could be as capable of sharing the inspiration of this important date with our campers."

The *shaliach* had always given priority to other peoples' needs, so he spent the night of *Yud-Beis Tammuz* with a group of campers, even though he had prepared to celebrate the chassidic holiday with the Rebbe.

A few days later, the Rebbe announced an unexpected *farbrengen* at "770". This was extremely uncommon in those years, and many wondered what was behind this unanticipated event. During the *farbrengen,* the Rebbe resolved their questions. "There is a *shaliach* who traveled here from afar," he explained, "and yet willingly forfeited his opportunity to spend *Yud-Beis Tammuz* at "770", so that he could hold a *farbrengen* with a group of campers. Now we are making it up to him."

The Previous Lubavitcher Rebbe, Rabbi Yosef Yitzchak Schneersohn, initiated the custom of dispatching groups of chassidim to *shuls* in various Jewish communities throughout New York City on the holidays. Despite the distance — it often involves hours of walking in each direction — the chassidim joyfully make the journey, sharing the spirit of the holiday and bringing a message from the Rebbe to the congregants whom they meet.

The scholar, Rabbi Nissan Telushkin, a Rabbi in a *shul* in East New York, greatly appreciated the visit by the chassidim. Shortly after the holiday one year, he was privileged to meet the Rebbe privately at *yechidus,* and he used the opportunity to thank him for sending the chassidim.

The Rebbe acknowledged his thanks saying, "Yes, it entails a measure of self-sacrifice on their part."

"Indeed," stated Rabbi Telushkin. "Hours of walking back and forth requires much self-sacrifice."

The Rebbe smiled. "There's a greater dimension of self-sacrifice: the readiness to extend oneself and reach out to others with the full knowledge that, at the very same time, a *farbrengen* is taking place at "770". To give up this opportunity and go to a different *shul* is a much greater self-sacrifice."

Very often the Rebbe's blessing to an individual or a group concludes with the phrase: *Azkir al hatziyun* — "I will mention this at the gravesite." Indeed, many times that phrase constitutes the entire reply.

The term *tziyon* refers to the grave of the Previous Rebbe — Rabbi Yosef Yitzchak Schneersohn — which is located in a Jewish cemetery in Queens, New York. The Rebbe frequently prays at the Previous Rebbe's gravesite. There he reads the multitude of letters that are sent to him from all over the world.

Many who have received this reply, unaware of the full implications of this phrase, may have desired "a more substantial blessing." Such was the case when Reb Shneur Zalman Duchman wrote to the Rebbe, asking for a blessing for a childless couple whom he knew. The Rebbe replied *Azkir al hatziyun.* Unsatisfied with this answer, Reb Shneur Zalman wrote a second note, asking the Rebbe to promise the couple a child. The reply was the same: *Azkir al hatziyun.* The reply was the same: *Azkir al hatziyun.*

Time passed. One day, just as the Rebbe was leaving his house, Reb Shneur Zalman was walking down President St. The Rebbe signaled to Reb Shneur Zalman to approach him.

"Have you heard that a son was born to the couple for whom you requested a blessing?" the Rebbe asked. "*Nu*, evidently *Azkir al hatziyun* has something to it."

* * *

We might gain some insight into the events which transpire while the Rebbe visits the Previous Rebbe's gravesite from an interchange between Rabbi Shmaryahu Gurary ע״ה, the Rebbe's brother-in-law, and Reb Azriel Zelig Slonim. Commonly known as the *Rashag*, Rabbi Gurary was an outstanding example of a chassid whose heart and soul were devoted to the Rebbe.

"As you know, Reb Zelig," explained the *Rashag.* "When my father-in-law, the Previous Rebbe, passed away, we were all heartbroken and confused. One day, I was deliberating unsuccessfully over a very important issue. I decided to consult my brother-in-law (the Rebbe *Shlita*).

"He weighed the matter carefully, and then said: 'I would not like to take personal responsibility for such an important issue. I will visit the gravesite later today, and I will discuss it with our father-in-law. Then I will give you an answer.' Upon his return, he presented me with an excellent solution."

"Now listen here, Reb Zelig," concluded the *Rashag.* "My brother-in-law is not one who exaggerates. If he said that he would discuss the matter with the Previous Rebbe at his gravesite, then that is exactly what transpired. I know that I am not capable of this. Since he can do so — I am his devoted chassid."

During the early years of the Rebbe's leadership, his *minyan* was graced by the presence of an illustrious personality, the revered Rebbe of Tomishpol-Koidenov, זצ״ל, who stood at the forefront of chassidic Rebbeim in America until his passing at the age of 108.

Once, the Rebbe *Shlita* returned late from praying at the *ohel*, the Previous Lubavitch Rebbe's gravesite. As he entered the *shul* for the afternoon service, he glanced at the Rebbe of Tomishpol and said: "A bit late?"

The Rebbe of Tomishpol replied: "There can be no more appropriate time for prayer than when the Rebbe *davens.*"

"I would like to share a personal experience with people who are disappointed at not having received answers to their letters to the Rebbe," relates a *chassid.* "I was accustomed to receiving answers to every letter which I sent the Rebbe. Then, almost abruptly, the replies stopped. As time passed, I decided to stop writing. If the Rebbe would not answer me, I saw no point in sending him letters.

Soon afterwards, I found a letter from "770" in my mailbox. I was amazed to find it handwritten by the Rebbe himself. It read: 'I am sorry that you misinterpreted the reasons for my lack of correspondence.' The Rebbe proceeded to explain that he had not responded, because of the heavy demands on his time."

Chapter 7 —
Yechidus

The word *yechidus* signifies a private meeting.
But for chassidim, the concept of a *yechidus* with a
Rebbe has a far deeper implication. The word
yechidah refers to the highest rung of the soul, the
innermost core which is at one with G-d in constant
and consummate unity. A *yechidus* with his Rebbe
— a one-to-one encounter between the *yechidah* of
the chassid and the *yechidah* of the Rebbe —
charges the chassid's *yechidah* with dynamism, so
that it vitalizes his day-to-day conduct.

"Of all my *yechidus* experiences," related Rabbi Yehudah Leib Posner, "the one I remember most wasn't only for me. During the Spring of 1965, I was assistant principal of an elementary school for girls in Vineland, New Jersey. I had been trying to direct the eighth grade graduates to enroll in religious high schools. I suggested that they visit New York City and acquaint themselves with the different educational opportunities available for them there: *Bais Rivkah*, the Lubavitch High School for girls, the *Beis Yaakov* schools, and others.

"I organized a trip to New York on Sunday with a stop in Crown Heights and a tour of the Lubavitch school. I then phoned the office at "770" and arranged with the secretary, Rabbi Shalom Mendel Simpson, to arrange that the girls meet the Rebbe at *yechidus* for the girls at 3:00 on Sunday.

"The trip was very pleasant, and at 2:45 on Sunday we were waiting outside "770". However, in the office I was told that the Rebbe had unintentionally not been informed of the arrangement. Rabbi Simpson asked us to wait a short while, and then announced that the girls would be able to see the Rebbe after *minchah* at 3:15.

"It was *Pesach Sheni*, the minor holiday instituted to enable all those who had not offered a sacrifice on Passover to compensate by bringing an offering on this date. The Rebbe spoke to the girls about the lesson one can learn from this holiday, that *Es iz nito kein farfal'n* — Nothing is ever lost; there is always an opportunity to compensate.

"After the Rebbe finished talking to the girls, I requested an opportunity for a personal *yechidus* and the Rebbe consented.

"Afterwards, I wondered how great an exception the Rebbe had made to grant the girls *yechidus* on such short notice. I was curious how far in advance it was necessary to schedule *yechidus*. I asked Rabbi Simpson if he could arrange a *yechidus* for me in the near future. Rabbi Simpson shook his head.

"'Of course, I don't mean tomorrow or the next day,' I said quickly, fully aware of the waiting line for *yechidus*. 'I had in mind about six weeks from today.'

Rabbi Simpson shook his head again. 'It's absolutely full. There are no openings until after Sukkos.'

"I understood something about the Rebbe's choice of priorities. For myself, I had been told that I would have to wait at least five months to be received at *yechidus*. But when six young girls might possibly be influenced in their choice of high school education, the Rebbe took time in mid-day to speak to them despite the lack of previous notification."

And the Rebbe's words made a difference. Most of the six girls decided to continue their Jewish education.

Back in the 'seventies, distraught parents often placed long-distance phone calls to Rabbi Chaim Yitzchak Drizin, the *shaliach* in Berkeley, California. They sought help in communicating with their children who had joined cults and communes, or who were drifting about on the permissive West Coast shores.

So he was not fazed when a worried father, Mr. Friedman, called from New York to ask for help in contacting his daughter, Adina.

"She's a lovely girl, a student at Columbia," Mr. Friedman's words tumbled out in confusion. "They're in Immigrant Gap, California now.... Our family tries to keep *Shabbos*... but her black boyfriend is a missionary Christian.... Tomorrow night, he's taking her to Hawaii to convert her to Christianity. I think she's only doing it to please him. Please help."

Rabbi Drizin promised that he would do what he could. However, it was Friday. He wasn't even sure that he could find Immigrant Gap.

"I hesitated," recalled Rabbi Drizin. "I had heard the town's name before and I believed that it was somewhere near Sacramento. But I had no address, I didn't want to run late shortly before *Shabbos*. Could I really influence a stranger and bring about a change on such a critical issue on one short visit?"

"Yet, I was prompted to go. I planned what I thought was enough time to get there and back, left another two hours for discussion, and an hour to get ready for *Shabbos*. Instinctively, I hurried over to the *Chabad* House to pick up my *tallis*. I brushed by a poster announcing our Saturday night program, and again reminded myself that I must be home for *Shabbos*.

"After setting out on my journey, I realized that I had miscalculated. Immigrant Gap was further than I thought, but I had already traveled so far that I could not turn back. I arrived at five thirty, only a few hours before sunset. The residents of the tiny village could not direct me to the person I described. Realizing that I would have to stay here over *Shabbos*, I notified my family and then bought some kosher food. Finally, after an intense search, I located the people in a cottage atop a hill on the outskirts of town.

"It was just a few minutes before *Shabbos* when I knocked on the door. The owners, a devout Christian family, invited me in, and I saw their guests — the man and woman in the dining room — Adina and her friend. I introduced myself and told Adina the purpose of my visit. She showed no interest and left the room. Her missionary companion, in contrast, was more friendly. Perhaps he thought I would be an interesting challenge.

"I asked the houseowners if I could spend the night and the next day. They cordially offered me a spacious room.

"That *Shabbos* was quite an experience. Most of the day was spent in intense conversation. I often regretted being pitted against Adina, whose responses alternated between indifference and hostility. Instead of speaking to her directly, I spent most of the time speaking to her friend, trying to impress both of them with one concept: Before Adina should consider adopting a different religion, she should know more about her own.

"Late Saturday night, shortly before their scheduled flight to Hawaii, Adina surprised me by agreeing to attend a course on Judaism. I immediately placed two phone calls: one to Bais Chanah — a Lubavitch institute for girls in Minnesota — and the other to an airline ticket office. Early Sunday morning, I drove Adina to the airport in Sacramento.

"On the road, Adina broke the tense silence between us: 'I assure you, Rabbi, that you have no idea why I decided to accompany you. Not only that, but I'm sure that you have no idea what you are doing here in the first place!'

"Her outburst caught me unprepared. I had naively concluded that my extensive persuasion had finally borne fruit.

"'You see,' she continued, 'fifteen years ago, when I was growing up in New York, my father and I visited the Lubavitcher Rebbe. I did not understand what was being said at that meeting, but over the years, my father explained it to me.

"'While the Rebbe was granting us blessings, he stopped and said to my father: 'A day will come when you will need assistance with this child — contact us and we will help.'

"'Initially, I was not impressed when you introduced yourself on Friday as an emissary of the Lubavitcher Rebbe. Then, on Saturday, the profound prophecy of those words struck me. Nothing you said convinced me to change my plans. I still want to go to Hawaii, but I cannot disregard those far-sighted words of your Rebbe. I decided to go only out of respect for his profound vision.'

Today, Adina is the mother of a lovely, observant family in Jerusalem.

An Israeli police officer taking a professional training course in America decided to take advantage of his stay in the States in order to meet the Rebbe privately at *yechidus*. He handed the Rebbe a list of his family members, requesting a blessing for each of them.

After reading the note, the Rebbe asked: "How is your wife's leg?"

When the police officer simply responded with a blank look, the Rebbe gently reminded him about a letter that his son had written ten years earlier while attending a Lubavitch school.

When the child had been in third grade, the officer's wife had contracted a serious leg illness. The child's teacher saw his concern, and suggested that he write a letter to the Rebbe. Soon he received a blessing for a speedy recovery. In due time, his mother's leg healed.

In the interim, the officer and his family had moved to a different city, the children had grown up, and the officer had forgotten about the illness until now, when he was reminded by the Rebbe.

Later, the officer explained, "I do not know what is more moving to me: the fact that the Rebbe remembered after ten years and many thousands of other letters, or the genuine interest and care the Rebbe expressed for the well-being of another person."

One of the first students at the *Yeshivas Tomchei Temimim*, the *yeshivah* established in the village of Lubavitch in 1897 by the fifth Lubavitcher Rebbe, the Rashab, was Rabbi Shneur Zalman Gorelik, who later became the first *rav* of Kfar Chabad in Israel. Rabbi Gorelik assumed this position at the age of 70, following a lifetime of vibrant communal activity. He established and managed a *gemach*, free loan fund, from his own salary, thus helping many struggling immigrant families establish the future Lubavitch center in Israel.

Once Rabbi Gorelik confided in a friend, "Besides the *mitzvah* of offering free loans, the *gemach* helps me perform my rabbinical duties. You see, I am not young, and it is difficult for me to pay home visits as an active Rabbi should in our growing town.

"When people come for a loan, I can offer them assistance and guidance about their families, their finances, and their spiritual advancement.

But at his first *yechidus,* when he was already eighty years old, Rabbi Gorelik mentioned that the *gemach* required too much of his time.

The Rebbe replied, "To the contrary. The *gemach* grants you additional time." And Rabbi Gorelik was indeed granted much time, living well into his nineties.

At one point, Rabbi Gorelik told the Rebbe that he felt Kfar Chabad deserved a more dignified Rav. The Rebbe replied: "You can increase your dignity."

Professor Lombruzi is a prominent physicist who lives in Nice, France. He had become acquainted with Lubavitch, and once made a trip to New York to meet the Rebbe. Among the topics he discussed with the Rebbe during *yechidus* was a book on the subject of electricity. "I invested years of research and hard work in the publication, but it has not sold success-fully," he said disappointedly. As he spoke, Professor Lombruzi presented a copy of the book to the Rebbe as a gift.

The Rebbe leafed through the book for about a minute, and offered some constructive criticism. He suggested publish-ing a revised edition, promising that it and his subsequent works would gain a wide readership.

Many years have elapsed since the professor's first encounter with the Rebbe. He has published over twenty other volumes following his first book, and each one was a prodigious success. They have been translated into eight languages and have been chosen as compulsory texts in many major universities in France and other European countries. The title page of each book bears a dedication to the Lubavitcher Rebbe.

Curiosity, more than anything else, brought an Israeli journalist to *yechidus* in 1971. He had been visiting the States, and some of his American acquaintances said that they could arrange an encounter between him and the Rebbe.

Though he lacked the reverence of the Rebbe's followers, he appreciated the opportunity to meet such a great man. When the arranged date came, he entered the Rebbe's study and handed him a note with his questions and requests, as he had been advised.

The Rebbe gazed intently at the piece of paper. "I recognize this handwriting. You have written to me in the past," he said.

The journalist was taken aback by this unexpected comment. "With all due respect," he replied. "I have never written you a letter."

The Rebbe sat in deep thought for a few moments. "There is no doubt that you have written to me in the past," the Rebbe maintained. As he spoke, he opened the drawer of his desk, took out a piece of paper and handed it to the journalist.

The journalist stared at the paper, stunned. Here it was, a letter to the Rebbe written in his own handwriting. But what is this at the bottom? The letter was signed by someone else.

Then he remembered. A few years earlier, during the Six Day War, one of his buddies had injured his hand. After the war, the friend had wanted to send a letter to the Rebbe. Unfortunately, because of his injury, he was unable to write. The journalist wrote as his friend dictated, and the injured man managed to sign his name.

The journalist's attitude changed abruptly. The *yechidus* became far more than a curiosity, and he departed far less indifferent than when he had entered.

The Rebbe receives thousands of letters every week. Any letter which he decides to keep at hand must have a specific purpose.

"Upon the Rebbe's request, I delivered to his office forty volumes of scientific reports which I had prepared for the American Government. But I didn't really think he would take a look at them," related Dr. Velvel Green, a professor of microbiology. "After all, how would he find time to read through all this extensive research?"

Some months later, when the professor came to see the Rebbe for *yechidus,* the Rebbe noted that a conclusion reached in Volume 18 contradicted an assumption in Volume 38.[1]

---

1.   The Rebbe's ability to assimilate mathematical and scientific knowledge was noticed at a young age and was table-talk throughout Yekatrinoslav, the town where the Rebbe's father served as Rav.

Yeshayahu Sher, then a young lad who frequented the Schneerson home, studied privately with a noted engineer named Ostrovsky. He once told his teacher about the three gifted sons of Rabbi Levi Yitzchok Schneerson (the Rebbe's father — the Rebbe had two brothers; DovBer and Yisroel Aryeh Leib).

"Gifted, eh?" remarked the engineer. "Well, we shall see. I will write down a mathematical problem for you to present to them. If they can solve it, I will put their names on the university honors list!"

Yeshayahu delivered the equation to the boys and returned with their solutions a while later. Ostrovsky was amazed. "They are all correct," he announced. He set aside one of the papers. "This one displays the most concise and direct method of calculating the answer," he added. That paper was the Rebbe's.

Some time later, the headmaster of the local preparatory school visited the Schneerson home. He desired to test the reports he had heard about Rabbi Levi Yitzchok's oldest son. He presented the youth with a complex mathematical problem, allotting him three days to solve it. Half an hour later, while the head-

Migdal Ha'Emek is a development town in northern Israel. Anyone who meets Uzi Biton, the cook at the *Migdal Or* educational complex in that city, cannot see anything lacking in his manual ability. He effortlessly drags huge sacks of potatoes or large cartons of oranges around the campus kitchen.

"Look at the scar near my fingers," he points with a smile to his hand, which is stirring the contents of a huge pot. "I was wounded in the army. The palm of my hand was severely cut and the doctors told me that I had little chance of ever moving my fingers again. I underwent prolonged physical therapy to renew the blood flow, but to no avail. Having no other choice, I learned to live with my handicap.

"After my discharge from the army, I began to plan my future. During this time, I encountered *Chabad* and became more committed to Jewish life. Shortly afterwards, I decided to visit the Rebbe. In those days, it was still possible to have a private *yechidus*. As I prepared the note for *yechidus*, I wondered if I would be able to understand and remember everything the Rebbe would say. I decided to record the *yechidus* on a pocket tape recorder which I would place in my jacket pocket.

"The two points in my note to the Rebbe reflected the two issues which were of pressing importance in my life at that time: The first was the prospect of marriage. A young woman had already been introduced to me. The second, of course, was my handicap.

"The Rebbe read the note, marked it with a pencil, looked up at me, and said: 'Go ahead and propose marriage. Plan the wedding in the nearest possible future. And may G-d grant you a full recovery immediately.'

---

master was still speaking to Rabbi Levi Yitzchok, the youth returned with his answer. The headmaster considering him impudent at having worked on the problem so swiftly. He pocketed the paper without even looking at it.

At one-thirty in the morning, the telephone rang in the Schneerson home. "Please forgive me for calling at this unearthly hour," the headmaster said excitedly. "But I could not contain myself. Your son's solution to the problem I gave him is absolutely correct. I can't believe this; even an experienced mathematician would have taken three days to solve this problem."

"I fervently answered *Amen* and left the Rebbe's study. Outside, I was eager to review the Rebbe's words and reached into my pocket for the recorder. Suddenly, I realized to my amazement that my injured hand had removed the tape recorder — a feat previously unthinkable! The Rebbe's blessing for immediate recovery had been fulfilled in the most literal sense.

"His advice about marriage also taught me about the Rebbe's far-reaching vision and precision of words. I proposed to my wife shortly after my return, and plans were made for the wedding. Nevertheless, for various reasons, the wedding did not take place "in the nearest possible future." Shortly afterwards, my fiancee's father passed away. Not only did he did not merit to see his daughter married, but we had to postpone the emarriage until after the year of mourning."

Chapter 8 —
Farbrengen

In Yiddish, the word *farbrengen* means
"spending time together." It has come to describe an
earnest and brotherly gathering of chassidim,
punctuated by song and talk. When the Rebbe leads
a *farbrengen*, it takes on a more formal atmosphere
as he addresses his assembled followers,
communicating his Torah thoughts and his
messages for the Jewish world at large.

Although the Rebbe would speak at such
gatherings for several hours, he would share more
than the content. For the individuals present and for
the community at large, a *farbrengen* with the
Rebbe is a live experience. And it is some of that
vitality which we have tried to capture in the stories
that follow.

The *Rosh Yeshivah* apologized to his host, Rabbi Berl Rivkin, where he stayed when visiting New York. Although he shared family ties with his host, he nonetheless did not share all of Rabbi Rivkin's interests.

"Yes, I enjoyed the *davening* at "770" last night and this morning. Thank you for inviting me. But *farbrengens* are not for me. I'm not trying to minimize the depth and breadth of the Rebbe's scholarship, but his style and selection of topics are different from those discussed in our *yeshivah* world.

"I like to spend *Shabbos* afternoons embroiled in a complicated *Halachic* text or unraveling a difficult passage in the *Rambam's* works. Besides, I'm just not used to the Rebbe's style of exposition of *Rashi's* Torah commentary."

Rabbi Rivkin did not wish to press his guest. They spent the rest of the *Shabbos* meal discussing a complex passage of the *Rambam*. As the *farbrengen* was about to begin, Rabbi Rivkin left his guest grappling with the *Rambam* and hurried to "770". He made it to his place as the Rebbe was entering the hall.

The *farbrengen* began as usual, and the Rebbe elaborated on the lessons to be derived from the weekly Torah portion and the spiritual significance of this *Shabbos*, continuing with a deep chassidic discourse and lively singing.

During the singing, Rabbi Rivkin noticed his guest inching through the crowd. Evidently, the *Rosh Yeshivah* had decided to attend the *farbrengen*, and the chassidim were helping him reach his host's place. The Rebbe then began discussing *Rashi's* commentary.

Towards the conclusion of this talk, the Rebbe explained: "In light of all the above, one can also explain a difficult passage in the *Rambam*...." Rabbi Rivkin and his guest exchanged glances. This was the very passage which they had been studying. The *Rosh Yeshivah* leaned forward to hear every word.

He was astounded to hear the Rebbe clarify the difficulty in a few carefully worded sentences. He was equally overwhelmed that the Rebbe had tied this seemingly unrelated passage to his discussion just at the time that he had arrived at the *farbrengen*.

Still intrigued by this awesome coincidence, the *Rosh Yeshivah* was further surprised when, after concluding, the Rebbe turned to him with a smile and said, "There's no need to be astonished."

At the close of each Jewish holiday, the Rebbe *Shlita* holds a *farbrengen*. Afterwards, he recites the Grace After Meals, joins in the evening service, and then says *Havdalah*. The chassidim then file past and the Rebbe pours a little wine from the cup of wine used for both Grace and *Havdalah*, "the cup of blessing." An announcement is customarily made after the conclusion of the *farbrengen* for the benefit of the many visitors.

After the *farbrengen* which followed the second day of Rosh HaShanah, 5725, Rabbi Shneur Zalman Duchman made the familiar announcement. "The procedure will be as follows," he proclaimed. "After *Maariv*, the Rebbe will recite *Havdalah*, and then he will distribute wine from the 'cup of blessing.' The new *Vaad HaMesader* (organizing committee) asks everyone to proceed to receive the wine in an orderly manner."

The Rebbe smiled broadly and altered the announcement, addressing the directives to G-d as much as to the assembled: "The procedure will be as follows: First we will begin the new year, which will be accompanied by abundant goodness. Afterwards, we will immerse ourselves in the study of Torah, both *nigleh* (the revealed dimension of Torah law) and *chassidus* (its inner mystical secrets). We will then observe the *mitzvos* in a meticulous way.

"Even before we begin, G-d will have already inscribed us for a good and sweet year in every aspect of our lives, with blessings for our children and grandchildren, for success and prosperity; and for a good year in both a spiritual and physical sense. These," the Rebbe concluded, "are the recommendations of the new *Vaad HaMesader*, which all should follow."

A farbrengen in "770" is a multidimensional experience. The Rebbe is noticeably more intense just before delivering a *maamar*, formal chassidic discourse. In the middle of singing a chassidic *niggun*, his face becomes extremely serious, and everyone immediately changes the *niggun* to begin the traditional chassidic melody sung before *maamarim*.

In the very first years of the Rebbe's leadership, these signs were even more noticeable. In particular, the Purim *farbrengen* of 1953 stands out in the memory of many chassidim. At the beginning of the *farbrengen*, the Rebbe delivered a *maamar*. As usual, his deep concentration was visible throughout the entire prelude. After the *maamar*, the Rebbe delivered several addresses punctuated by chassidic song.

The *farbrengen* increased in intensity, continuing well past midnight. At this late hour, an elder chassid Reb Shmuel Levitin approached the Rebbe with a sincere request for a blessing for the welfare of the Jews in Russia.

Quite unexpectedly, after answering Reb Shmuel, the Rebbe showed visible signs of delivering another *maamar*. This was most unusual, as the Rebbe had never delivered two chassidic discourses during a single *farbrengen*. As the chassidim stood in anticipation of the *maamar*, the Rebbe related the following story:

"After the fall of the Czarist regime, general elections were held in Russia. The Rebbe Rashab, Rabbi Sholom Ber Schneersohn, instructed his followers to exercise their right to vote. The Rebbe's message was spread throughout the chassidic community. One chassid, a devout man who spent most of his time in pursuit of spiritual matters, was totally uninvolved in the country's politics. Nevertheless, he was prepared to carry out this directive as readily and intently as any of the Rebbe's other biddings.

"He immersed himself in the *mikveh*, girded his *gartel* (prayer belt) and proceeded to the polls. He was not familiar with the procedure, and did not even know for whom to vote. Luckily, he met other chassidim at the polls and they instructed him. With earnest concentration, the chassid adjusted his *gartel* and solemnly cast his ballot.

"As he glanced around him, he noticed many excited voters cheering for their candidate, shouting 'Hoo-rah! Hoo-rah!' The chassid thought that the chanting might be a required part of the voting procedure. Fearful that he might offend others or draw attention to himself if he refrained, he also joined the chanting.

"Hoo-rah is the Russian version of our familiar "hurray," but in Hebrew the words '*hoo rah*' mean 'he is evil.' So the chassid chanted, '*hoo rah*' along with the others, his intention being that he (the voters' hero) is evil."

With this the Rebbe concluded the story. The crowd in "770" also began to chant, "Hoo rah, hoo rah."

After the *farbrengen* there was much discussion among the chassidim regarding the unexpected *maamar* and the preceding story. Everyone sensed that it was somehow related to events taking place somewhere behind the Iron Curtain.

Soon afterwards, the news hit the headlines. The infamous Russian ruler Stalin had suffered a fatal stroke.

"It's more than just a desire to prolong the holiday spirit," the man from Boro Park said to his fellow passenger, riding to Crown Heights on the night following the last day of Passover. "It's quite exhilarating to enter "770", where thousands of people are still celebrating the holiday, as opposed to my community, where everyone hurries home after *Havdalah* to put away the Pesach dishes.

"But I don't come just for the inspiration. I make this trip after every holiday when the Rebbe distributes some of the "cup of blessing" after *Havdalah*. I've heard of numerous miraculous incidents occurring at these occasions."

The two men stood in line, waiting together with the thousands of others to approach the Rebbe. After the first one received his wine, the second held out a small cup to receive wine from the Rebbe. Instead of pouring, the Rebbe motioned to the man to hold the cup with his right hand.

The man made no move to exchange hands and the Rebbe did not pour the wine. An attendant urged him: "*Reb Yid*, please hold the cup in your right hand."

With obvious trepidation, the man extended his right hand. He looked on in disbelief as the Rebbe filled his cup. The people around him were almost annoyed with the delay he had caused the Rebbe. But he wholeheartedly forgave them. How could they have known that his right hand had been paralyzed?

"I suppose I should have felt thankful and lucky," relates Reb Feivel, speaking about his involvement in rehabilitating displaced Jews in post-war Europe. "I found it difficult to be optimistic about life after I had lost everything in the Holocaust. An old friend of mine found me a job in the *Vaad HaHatzalah* (Rescue Organization) offices in Paris. My heavy workload helped me maintain my sanity.

"Sitting behind a big gray desk piled with papers, files, and forms, I found solace in being in a position to help others reconstruct their lives, yet I also felt constant misery while listening to tale after tale of woe.

"One day, I heard a short, gentle knock at my office door. This was a pleasant change from the familiar nervous rapping of troubled survivors.

'Come in,' I called.

"A well-dressed, bearded, man walked up to my desk. His distinguished features radiated inner peace. That over-whelmed me, for in post-war Europe inner peace was a very rare commodity. Moreover, his peaceful composure was infectious, and for the first time in years, I felt at ease.

'How can I help you?' I asked.

'My mother, Rebbetzin Chanah Schneerson has arrived here from Russia. I have come to facilitate her immigration to the United States. Can you please advise me how much time I will have to set aside for this procedure? I would like to organ-ize my schedule accordingly.'

"I could not take my eyes of this softly-spoken man. He was the first person who came through my office who radiated a sense of direction, expressing the desire to calculate time and spend it wisely. In the shambles of a chaotic Europe, this man valued his minutes.

"I promised to assist him, assuring him that I would process the necessary papers myself so that he could use his time as he saw fit. I gave him the necessary forms, and he supplied the information. Afterwards, he expressed his gratitude and left my office. Though I had not said so, I was also grateful to him. The few minutes he had spent with me endowed me with renewed dedication and sense of purpose.

"Many years passed. In the interim, I had married, built a family and immigrated to the States. One day, I was driving through Brooklyn with a co-worker. 'Let's go visit the Lubavitch Headquarters,' he suggested. 'Why not?' I replied. Seventeen years had passed since that incident in Paris. Although I had never gone to see the Rebbe, I had since learned that he was the man who had visited my office then and that meeting was still etched in my memory.

"We arrived at "770" in the midst of a *farbrengen*. I marveled at the atmosphere of spiritual intensity, which sharply contrasted with the ordinary American environment. I looked around slowly, shifting my eyes from the Rebbe to the chassidim periodically.

"Suddenly, I caught the Rebbe's eye, and he caught mine. He looked at me directly, and then said something to an attendant. Before I knew it, the attendant was beside me. 'The Rebbe has requested that you come,' he whispered to me. I was both surprised and flustered at the unexpected attention.

"I nervously followed the attendant and found myself face to face with the Rebbe. It was the same warm and eloquent voice that had echoed in my ears seventeen years ago. 'Yasher Koach for your efforts on behalf of my mother in Paris. Blessings and thanks for everything you did.'"

Among the participants of a *Shabbos farbrengen* in the spring of 1952 was the world chess champion, Mr. Roshevsky. At one point during the talks, the Rebbe explained that anything can teach people lessons in serving G-d. He then related the following story.

It is customary to refrain from Torah study on the eve of December 25.[1] One such evening, the fifth Lubavitcher Rebbe, the Rebbe Rashab, saw his son, Yosef Yitzchak (who later succeeded him as Rebbe) playing chess with a revered chassid, Reb Elchanon Dov Morozov.

The Rebbe Rashab stood nearby and said: "*Nu*, it is not fair to give advice." He watched the game without uttering a word. Afterwards, the Rebbe proceeded to teach a lesson in worshipping G-d based upon the game of chess, explaining that there are two kinds of chess pieces: the officers and the simple soldiers, the pawns.

---

1. See *Sefer HaMinhagim* (English translation, Kehot, N.Y., 1992), p. 162.

The officers may make a variety of different moves and move several squares at a time. The pawns, by contrast, may only progress one square at a time. Nevertheless, when the pawn arrives at the other end of the board, he may ascend in rank and may be exchanged for any other piece, even a queen. However, a pawn cannot assume the rank of a king, for there is only one king.

Our worship of G-d is similar. There are heavenly angels and mortal men. The angels, like the officers in the game of chess, have a wide range of movement which is unrestricted by physical limitations. However, their rank and level can never change. Mortals, on the other hand, are like pawns. They can progress only one step at a time. Yet, when these souls complete their mission in this world and "reach the other side," they can assume higher ranks, even becoming "queens." Still, there is only one king — the King of Kings, the Holy One, blessed be He.

Chapter 9 —
A Dollar for Tzedakah —
A Fountain of Blessing

It was the Rebbe's birthday, Sunday, the 11th of Nissan, 5746. As the chassidim were finishing their morning prayers, word spread through the *shul:* "The Rebbe is giving out dollars for *tzedakah* at the door of his study!" And within moments a line of hundreds formed. One by one, they filed past the Rebbe and each received a brief blessing and a dollar to be given to charity.

Two weeks later, after the Pesach holiday, the scene replayed itself, and on the following Sunday weeks later, the chassidim were no longer surprised.

This marked the beginning of an institution that was to give tens of thousands of people from all over the world an opportunity to establish a connection with the Rebbe. From that first Sunday until Sunday, the 26th of Adar, 5752 (the day before the Rebbe suffered the stroke from which he is presently recovering), week after week, the Rebbe would stand in the entrance hall of "770" for hours on end, receiving people from all walks of life and giving them dollars to distribute for charity.

Every week thousands would come. Some came asking for blessings at a turning-point in their lives, others came because of a problem, and still others in search of spiritual inspiration. There were probably as many reasons as there were people on the line.

The people represented a true cross-section of the international Jewish community: venerable sages, young children, communal leaders, visitors from every country in the world, the observant and the not-yet-observant, political figures from the U.S. and Israel, and *amcha Yidden*, the Jewish man-in-the-street, in his thousands.

A friend from Israel once visited "770" for Shavuos. That year, the holiday was celebrated on Sunday and Monday, and so the Rebbe did not distribute dollars that Sunday morning. "One of the most striking experiences of my trip," my friend recalls, "was to see Jews who came to "770" with the intent of receiving dollars that Sunday. These people who obviously were not aware of the holiday celebrating the Giving of the Torah were eager to receive the Rebbe's blessing."

"Pardon me," said the visitor to the man standing in front of him. They were both waiting on line to receive a dollar from the Rebbe on a spring Sunday.

The man in front of him turned around. "How can I help you?" he asked pleasantly.

"This is the first time I've come and I'm not quite sure how to approach the Rebbe," the newcomer continued. "You see, I'm having severe difficulty with my youngest son. He is going through an extremely rebellious period. I would like to request the Rebbe's blessing on this matter.

"Would you be able to assist me in the proper wording. I understand one must be short and precise and I would not like to take too much precious time from the Rebbe."

The man thought for a moment and then said to the visitor. "You seem to understand the need to keep the line moving. Imagine how many more hours the Rebbe would have to stand here if every person would speak to him, even briefly. So, the Rebbe's blessing of *Brochah v'hatzlachah* ('blessing and success') to each person as he hands him the dollar includes all his needs."

The newcomer understood and decided not to mention anything to the Rebbe. As the Rebbe handed him the dollar, he listened wholeheartedly to the anticipated *Brochah v'hatzlachah*. He felt the blessing empower him with faith and strength. As he moved on, he suddenly realized that the Rebbe had not turned to the person behind him, but instead was beckoning him to wait.

The Rebbe handed him an additional dollar, saying: "For your son."

❧

"I didn't know the Lubavitcher Rebbe knew you!" exclaimed Mrs. Berkowitz to her husband. She was waving two dollars in her hand. Rabbi Berkowitz, a prominent lecturer (*maggid shiur*) in a Brooklyn *yeshivah* looked at his wife quizzically.

"I went to receive a blessing from the Rebbe. The Rebbe handed me an additional dollar. 'This is for your husband,' he said. 'Tell him that I asked about him and that I send him my regards.'"

Mrs. Berkowitz handed her husband the dollar bill, but he wasn't paying attention. With a distant look in his eyes, he mumbled, "The Rebbe remembered... thirty years ago... that's amazing...."

Rabbi Berkowitz seemed very intent as he related an incident which had taken place three decades earlier. "It was during the summer month of Tammuz," he recalled. "I was walking down President Street towards Brooklyn Ave. A bearded man who just turned the corner caught my attention. He had very dignified features, his appearance was most impressive, and he was walking briskly. I stopped to have a chat with him. We exchanged some Torah thoughts and opinions about current events.

"As our conversation ended, the gentleman invited me to attend a chassidic *farbrengen* which was to be held by the Lubavitcher Rebbe in a couple of days. Although I knew very little about the Rebbe in those days, I decided to attend.

"You can imagine how I felt when I entered the *shul* at "770" Eastern Parkway. The man with whom I had conversed was none other than the Rebbe himself.

"I regretted having wasted the Rebbe's precious time. Afterwards, I asked him to forgive me. The Rebbe assured me that I needn't worry. He welcomed me to come back more often. 'I will yet ask about you,' were the Rebbe's parting words."

"I never returned," said Rabbi Berkowitz softly. "Today was the first time in thirty years that anyone in our family has gone to see the Rebbe."

❧

"I was sure the Rebbe had not heard correctly," related Y. Shifrin, a visitor to New York from Bnei Brak, Israel. "It was Sunday; I had joined the line at "770" to request a blessing from the Rebbe for a book I was about to publish. In response, the Rebbe gave me an additional dollar and said: 'Give *tzedakah* for her merit, and may she have a quick recovery.'

"I was mystified. Before I could collect my thoughts, the line had proceeded further. I was convinced that the Rebbe had not heard my request properly. I traveled back to my hosts' home in Boro Park, only to be greeted with an urgent message. 'Your wife called from Israel. She wants you to contact home immediately.'

"Anxiously, I placed the call. One of my daughters answered the phone, explaining that my wife was not home. 'She is at the hospital,' she said. My heart skipped a beat as the events unfolded. My youngest daughter who was in an advanced stage of pregnancy had lost consciousness and collapsed. The doctors described her condition as critical.

"With a jolt, the Rebbe's words flashed through my mind. A deep sense of calm settled within me. I told my daughter of the encounter which had occurred only a short while earlier and tried to reassure her. 'I'm sure everything will be fine.'

"I immediately gave *tzedakah* in my daughter's merit. That evening, my wife called again. 'The doctors have no explanation, but, thank G-d, the crisis has passed.'"

❧

Two of the taxi passengers *en route* from Ben Gurion airport to Jerusalem struck up a casual conversation. Following the friendly "Jewish geography" exchange in which one of the travelers introduced himself as a Jew from Antwerp, his new acquaintance, a Jerusalemite, continued with the common question, "What brings you here?"

The man from Antwerp hesitated for a moment. His European nature was not as open and uninhibited as the Israeli's. But somehow, his fellow passenger put him at ease.

"I'll tell you the truth," began the visitor. "This past summer on a trip to New York, I traveled to Brooklyn to ask the Lubavitcher Rebbe for a blessing for my handicapped son. We have had great difficulty finding a suitable match for him. As I passed by the Rebbe, he handed me a dollar saying *b'suros tovos* — good tidings. Then he gave me an additional dollar and said: 'For *tzedakah* in the Holy Land.'

"I was sure that the Rebbe had mistakenly thought I was a visitor from Israel. I didn't understand how this response applied to me, and I returned to Antwerp. Weeks passed and the holidays arrived. One day, during *Chol Hamoed Sukkos,* my wife and I were discussing our family affairs. We were both very concerned about the future of our son, who was not getting any younger. During the course of our conversation, my encounter with the Rebbe came up.

"My wife became thoughtful. 'Perhaps we should have taken the Rebbe's words more seriously,' she suggested. 'Let's follow his directive. Take a few days off after the holiday and travel to Israel to give *tzedakah* in the Holy Land, just as the Rebbe had said.'

"This is the reason for my journey," he concluded.

The visitor from Antwerp had been casting his eyes on the scenery as he told his story. It was only now that he noticed a strange mixture of awe and nervousness on the Jerusalemite's face.

"I wonder," the man was mumbling, unable to hide his excitement. Responding to the visitor's puzzled look, the man from Jerusalem struggled to regain his composure and related: "I am returning from a trip to New York, where I spent the holidays. I took the opportunity to ask the Rebbe for a blessing for my daughter. We would very much like to see her happily married. The Rebbe gave me a slice of *lekach* (honey cake) for my daughter saying: 'May she find a good *shiduch* (match) in the near future.'

The man from Jerusalem took a deep breath. "Perhaps we should both pursue the issue. You see, my daughter also has a handicap."

The engagement party was held shortly thereafter.

"It was a pleasant Sunday morning in July, 1988. I should have felt as content and relaxed as any other mother of a six-week-old beautiful baby girl. The baby still had the precious delicacy of a newborn, and yet had begun to develop a schedule which allowed the new mother more rest and renewed strength.

"Yet, I was tense and worried. The results of my post-partum examination had shattered my hopes and plans for my family of four lovely children. "A cancerous illness," the doctors said. As I sat there with numbing fear, I could hear them say something about an urgent operation because of the critical stage of the illness. I couldn't believe they were talking about me.

"That sunny Sunday morning appeared to me as a ray of hope. Before consulting the doctor again, I decided to pay a visit to "770" and speak to the Rebbe as he distributes dollars to be given to charity.

"I asked a neighbor to accompany me. 'I'm nervous, I feel weak, and I don't even speak Yiddish,' I told her. She readily agreed to come.

"As we approached the Rebbe, my neighbor related my desperate condition: 'The doctors say they have found cancer.'

"'So they will lose it!' the Rebbe responded, his face breaking into a broad smile.

"We were stunned. The Rebbe's matter-of-fact answer had caught us both off guard and in our confusion, we thought we had not heard correctly.

"'What?' we both burst out.

"The Rebbe was still smiling. 'You told me what they found. *Nu*, so whatever they found, they will lose.'

"By this time, I had grasped the Rebbe's words and I was overcome with emotion. "I have a six-week-old baby," I blurted tearfully in English.

"The Rebbe looked at me warmly and said: "You will merit to raise her to Torah, *chuppah* (marriage), and good deeds."

Shortly afterwards, the doctors indeed told the woman about a loss — one that she and her family were very relieved to hear.

One hot Sunday afternoon in the summer of 1991, an elderly lady was patiently waiting her turn in the long line of Jewish women and girls from all walks of life, each one anticipating the moment of receiving the Rebbe's blessing and the dollar bill to be given to *tzedakah*.

When her turn finally arrived, this lady blurted out in her simple Yiddish, "Rebbe! I've been standing here for only an hour and I'm already exhausted. You have been standing here for hours and hours, and just look....!"

The Rebbe smiled gently and said, "When you are counting diamonds, you don't get tired."

Chapter 10 —
A Great Treasure

The Rebbe *Shlita* has explained that having
children — and many children — is one of the
greatest treasures that can be granted a family. And
in many instances, his blessings have helped
childless families bring children into the world.

Mrs. Cheyena Avtzon had given birth to six children in Europe. When she and her husband, Rabbi Meir Avtzon, came to the U.S., she expected to receive a more advance and patient-oriented approach to medical treatment.

How surprised was she that upon a visit to a gynecologist, he adamantly told her she should never consider having another child!

Mrs. Avtzon tenaciously told the doctor that his job was to help women have children, not to count them or try to prevent them from having more. When she told the Rebbe *Shlita* about the doctor's prognosis of the dangers that might arise in future pregnancies, the Rebbe *Shlita* answered with a vigorous blessing, promising her that she would have many more children.

Which she did. Nine more children subsequently joined the Avtzon family.

In 1981, the Rebbe *Shlita* spoke publicly about the importance of having large families in his address to the Convention of the Lubavitch Women's Organization. Afterwards, it was decided that the Convention be closed with an address from a women who grew up in a large family. And it was no surprise that one of Mrs. Avtzon's daughters was the one chosen to give the address.

For many, the financial burden of raising children can be as challenging as bearing them. During one *yechidus*, Rabbi Avtzon told the Rebbe that his children were reaching marriageable age. He and his wife had never worried about their own finances, but he wanted to be able to provide the children with at least a modest wedding and dowry.

The Rebbe replied, "Material *nadden* (dowry) comes and goes; spiritual *nadden* stays forever. G-d gave you the unique gift to offer your children spiritual *nadden*. This is genuine *nadden.* You can tell this to your prospective in-laws in my name when you sit down to discuss the wedding details."

"Many of the people living in the large Jewish community of Monsey, New York, are native New Yorkers," says Mr. Klein. "I dare say I represent a large proportion of the people living in Monsey who do not miss the Big Apple at all. There are, however, attractions in the city which are close to our hearts. Although I am not a Lubavitcher, one of the things which I try not to miss when I'm in the city is the chance to receive a dollar from the Rebbe on Sunday mornings.

"I wanted to share this uplifting experience with my neighbors, a couple who had been married for fifteen years without children. At first the couple, affiliated with the Satmar chassidim, were reluctant to consider the option. Eventually, however, the woman decided she would make the trip to New York and seek the Rebbe's blessing.

"When she returned, the woman disappointedly told my wife, 'If this was an opportunity to receive a blessing from a *tzaddik,* then I must have forfeited it.'

" 'What happened?' asked my wife.

" 'I arrived at "770",' the woman explained. "The line of women was very long, so I had ample time to consider how to phrase my request. However, when I finally reached the Rebbe. I was so overwhelmed by the Rebbe's awesome personality that I could not utter a word.

" 'The Rebbe handed me a dollar and said, *Brochah v'hatzlachah* (blessing and success). Then he gave me another two dollars saying: These are for the children.

" 'That was that. I was so excited, I didn't open my mouth and I never got the blessing.'

"My wife eagerly responded, 'What do you mean, you never got the blessing?' she cried excitedly. 'You received a great blessing! The Rebbe gave you two dollars for the children you will have!'

"The woman shrugged, 'The Rebbe didn't specifically bless me to have children. I'm sure he routinely gives Jewish women additional dollars for their children.'

"It took some convincing to explain otherwise. However, exactly nine months later there was no need to convince anyone. The woman gave birth to twins."

"No, I'm not a follower of the Rebbe," the scholarly looking man confided in me. "As a matter of fact I am the head of a *Kollel* (an intensive adult Torah study program) and my lifestyle is far from chassidic. But I do recognize greatness...."

I sat back to listen as the man related his tale:

"I was born in Paris after World War II, about forty-five years ago. I remained an only son, as my parents were already middle-aged. Even when I was young, I sensed that my parents were withholding some secret about my birth.

I became engaged at the age of twenty-four. A short while before my wedding, my father, may he rest in peace, disclosed the story. I can still see him, as he sat close to me, with tears coming to his eyes when he lifted the veil of confidence from his long-kept secret.

"My parents were among the *lucky* Polish Jews who escaped to Russia during World War II. They joined bands of homeless refugees who wandered from place to place until they arrived in the city of Tashkent in the Carpathian Mountains. Tashkent was a temporary haven for refugees, including many Lubavitcher chassidim.

"My father always spoke highly of the Lubavitchers whom he had met in Tashkent. Self-sacrifice was their way of life. They offered assistance and support beyond their means. Their prayers reflected a deep commitment to Judaism. But most outstanding was their intense struggle to educate the young, despite their hardships during those difficult years."

My acquaintance paused, as if he was reflecting upon his father's tale, and then he returned to his story:

"My father was already nearly fifty years old, and my mother was about forty, when the war ended. They wanted to establish a home. Fortunately, being Polish citizens, they were able to leave Russia. They mingled with the migrating masses who were crossing Europe, and eventually made their home in Paris. They were grateful for having survived, but they faced the pain of childlessness after twenty years of marriage.

"In those days, Paris was a melting pot of refugees, and my parents were delighted to come across former acquaintances. Among them were some Lubavitcher chassidim whom they had befriended in Tashkent.

"One day, shortly after my parents arrived in Paris, my father met a beaming Lubavitcher chassid. 'We've merited a great guest in town. Rabbi Schneerson, the son-in-law of the Lubavitcher Rebbe, has arrived in Paris. He came to welcome his mother, Rebbetzin Chanah Schneerson ע״ה, who just left Russia.'

"On several occasions, my father met Rabbi Schneerson in the *shul* at the *Pletzel* in Paris and talked with him. My father was a learned scholar, and he cherished these talks with Rabbi Schneerson. During one of those conversations, Rabbi Schneerson inquired about my father's experiences during the war. When he touched upon the topic of family, my father tearfully explained that he did not have children.

"With compassion in eyes, Rabbi Schneerson gripped my father's hand warmly, and blessed him, 'May G-d enable you to fulfill the *mitzvah* of *Vehigadeta levincha* ("Relate to your children...")[1] next year.'

"The following year, I was two months old when *Pesach* approached. Two more years passed, and my parents emigrated from Europe to Israel. From the time I can remember, the *Seder* has always been an emotional experience for my father. He always expounded upon *avadim hayinu*[2] patiently, extensively, and with much love and joy.

"I could not appreciate my father's intensity at the *Seder* until he disclosed the story of my birth."

My acquaintance was visibly moved as he retold his father's story. I could see his eyes glistening at the edges. Before I could think of an appropriate response, he waved his hand as if beckoning me not to interrupt.

"And that's not all," he exclaimed. "Three years ago, my daughter married a *yeshivah* student from Lakewood, New Jersey. She was due to give birth the following Pesach. We had planned a family trip to the States to spend the holiday together, and celebrate the arrival of our grandchild. My wife arrived a month earlier to assist my daughter, while my younger children and I arrived in New Jersey a week before Pesach.

"At that time, I told my son-in-law, 'I would like to see the Lubavitcher Rebbe and have my younger son receive his blessing.'

"My son-in-law was less enthusiastic. His home community did not have many followers of the Rebbe, and he felt no need to make the two-hour journey. I, however, was not to be dissuaded. When my son-in-law saw that I was intent on going, he told me about the opportunity to meet briefly with the Rebbe on Sunday morning, when the Rebbe distributes dollars

---

1. The Biblical phrase *(Exodus* 13:8) commanding Jews to tell the story of the Pesach miracle.
2. The response to the Four Questions asked by a child during the *Seder.*

to be given to charity. I readily agreed, and my son-in-law arranged a ride into Brooklyn for me and my young son.

"We neared "770", and we were amazed to see a winding, block-long line of people waiting to see the Rebbe. During those hours in which we waited our turn, I told the miraculous story of my birth to my son.

"He was very moved to hear the story. 'I was surprised that you were so determined to come here," he said, "and I did not know why you were willing to wait so long. Time has always been very precious to you. Now I understand.'

"Finally, after hours of slowly inching forward, we reached a point from where we could see the distinguished and impressive appearance of the Rebbe. There was a tangible spirit of divinity in the air. I was amazed at the Rebbe's alertness, despite many hours of speaking to the thousands of people who passed by. He blessed each one and handed out *tzedakah* personally.

"Though the line of people passed quickly, I could see that some of them said something to the Rebbe and that he responded. I hadn't planned to say anything. I just wanted to see and approach the Rebbe once. 'Maybe it was my personal need to thank him for the blessing that he gave my parents, which culminated in my birth,' I thought to myself.

"Our turn arrived more quickly than I had anticipated. The Rebbe gave my son, who was standing before me, a dollar. *Brochah v'hatzlachah,* the Rebbe said. Then he asked him in Yiddish. 'Are you ready to ask the Four Questions?' My son was caught by surprise, not having expected the Rebbe to address him. Sensing his surprise, the attendant explained the question.

"My son regained his composure and responded, 'Yes.' The Rebbe smiled and handed him another dollar. 'This is for the Four Questions' he said.

"As I approached the Rebbe, he handed me a dollar saying: *'Brochah v'hatzlachah.'* He handed me a second dollar, 'for the answer to the Four Questions.' Then he gave me a deeply penetrating look, and with a tremendous smile he added: 'And for *Vehigadeta levincha.'*"

Rabbi Elimelech Nieman is one of the leading communal figures in the Jewish community of Boro Park. He has a long relationship with the Rebbe and consults him on many issues.

Each year, he comes to the Rebbe on the day before Yom Kippur when the Rebbe distributes *lekach* (honey-cake) and gives blessings to his followers for the coming new year.

Once he took a friend who had been childless for several years after marriage. The Rebbe gave Rabbi Nieman's friend his customary blessing for a good and sweet year. The friend told the Rebbe he had no children.

The Rebbe replied, "I blessed you with 'A good and sweet year.' This includes children."

A little more than nine months later, the friend's wife gave birth.

"We want children very badly," the woman told her rabbi, Yossi Goldman, one of the Lubavitcher *shluchim* in South Africa. "I've already had one miscarriage, and the doctors are very pessimistic about my ability to carry through a successful pregnancy. We have looked into adopting a child and the agencies have located a boy for us. Should we adopt the child or endeavor to have her own?"

Rabbi Goldman had much experience in consulting families, but this was a responsibility that he did not want to accept alone. With tactful sensitivity, he helped the woman compose a letter to the Rebbe.

The Rebbe's answer was not long in coming: "You will be able to have your own child. There is no need for adoption."

Shortly afterwards, the woman became pregnant. In the nine months of pregnancy, many complications arose. Each time, she wrote to the Rebbe, and each time, the Rebbe replied with confidant assurance. Ultimately, she gave birth to a healthy baby.

"Approximately five years ago, when I was working at the Kingsbrook Medical Center in Brooklyn," relates Renee Javer, "I was given a copy of *L'Chaim*, a weekly Lubavitch newsletter, by some young boys who came to the hospital every Friday to lift the patients' spirits and to distribute literature.

"The publication was interesting, and I became a subscriber. This opened the door to a greater interest in Judaism and subsequently, I subscribed to other Lubavitch publications. After a number of years, a Lubavitcher outreach worker called and asked if I was interested in 'learning.' At that time, I had recently retired, my mother was severely ill, and I felt the need for spiritual guidance — I readily agreed.

"I was contacted by a very pleasant young woman and we studied together for several months. We exchanged more than knowledge and became close friends. At one point, she asked me to come to a Sunday brunch in Crown Heights to be held for women who had begun to participate in these study sessions. I was happy to attend.

"After the brunch, my friend asked me if I wanted to see the Rebbe. I had heard that every Sunday the Rebbe would distribute *tzedakah*, but had never thought of going myself. After a word of gentle persuasion, I decided to join the line.

While we were waiting in front of "770", my emotions began to mount. When I finally stood before the Rebbe, I was overtaken by awe. With tears in my eyes, I told him that my daughter-in-law desired to have another child, but was encountering difficulty.

"'Think positively,' the Rebbe replied, assuring me that she would have a child.

"My friend arranged that a picture be taken of my meeting with the Rebbe. Thirteen months later, my daughter-in-law gave birth to a baby boy. Today, the two pictures — me and the Rebbe, and my daughter-in-law and her son — hang on my refrigerator door. When friends and family see them, they ask questions, and it brings on a wonderful discussion."

Chapter 11 —
The Quality of Mercy

When recalling his visits with other disciples at the court of his Rebbe, the Maggid of Mezritch, the Alter Rebbe would say, "When we were at the Maggid's table, miracles used to roll about freely on the floor; we didn't even bother to pick them up."

For forty-three years, miracles have rolled freely on the floor in "770" and yet, by and large, they were not picked up. Stories of miracles were told at chassidic gatherings, but they were never the focus of attention.

Why? — Because like the Maggid's disciples, the Rebbe's followers were much more involved with putting into practice the Rebbe's far-reaching vision, than relating the wonders that he brought about.

Why, then, are we now telling such stories? — To help us realize that our reality is not restricted to the limitations of our physical environment, and that there is more to our world than material substance and natural law.

In *Tanya*,[1] the Alter Rebbe cites a teaching of our Sages — "Originally, G-d thought to create the

---

1.   *Shaar HaYichud VehaEmunah*, ch. 5.

world with the attribute of stern judgment; He saw, however, that the world could not endure, so He blended it with the attribute of mercy" — and explains that the attribute of mercy refers to "the revelation of G-dliness through *tzaddikim*."

In order to enable us to appreciate the extent of our innate spiritual capacity, G-d grants us righteous men who are able to bring about change that defies the accustomed limits of nature.

This chapter relates many wondrous stories concerning health (thus directly relating to the quality of mercy mentioned in *Tanya*). At the same time, our Sages[2] advise us not to rely on miracles. Thus the chapter also includes several stories highlighting the practical advice that the Rebbe most often gives with regard to health problems: to provide a natural conduit for Divine blessings, consult a doctor who is a friend.

---

2. *Pesachim* 64b.

On the fifteenth of Elul, in 1970, the entrance to "770" was crowded with the members of the families of the groom and bride who were to be married several hours afterwards. They had come several hours early in order to receive the Rebbe's blessing as he went from *minchah* to his study. Unexpectedly, he gazed intently at the groom's father, Rabbi Zalman Leib Astulin of Bnei Brak, Israel, and ordered, "What is this? What is this? Go straight to a doctor!"

All those present were amazed by the Rebbe's sudden reaction. Only Rabbi Astulin comprehended that the Rebbe was addressing the condition of his leg.

During World War II, he had suffered a leg injury, and had to use crutches since. Lately, he had been suffering agonizing pain. Not wishing to disrupt the wedding preparations, which included a trip to New York and an opportunity to spend the festive month of Tishrei in "770", Rabbi Astulin had not mentioned his suffering to his family.

In response to the Rebbe's directive, he resolved to get medical attention as soon as he returned to Israel. "I do not know any doctors in New York," he thought. "Besides, I could never afford the doctors' fees here."

As he stood in thought, the Rebbe turned back and reprimanded, "Right away. Immediately! Before Rosh HaShanah!"

Caught off guard by the Rebbe's response to his thoughts, Rabbi Astulin blurted: "But I do not know anyone here."

"Dr. Seligson (the Rebbe's personal doctor) will refer you to the right physician," said the Rebbe.

After examining the leg, Dr. Seligson sensed the severity of the condition and referred Rabbi Astulin to Dr. Redler, an orthopedic specialist. A mere glance at the leg was sufficient for Dr. Redler to recoil in sympathy and pessimism. "I'm terribly sorry. There is a severe infection and irreversible gangrene. I cannot help you." The x-rays supported his diagnosis. "There's nothing I can do. There is no healthy tissue left. It's decayed entirely."

Mrs. Astulin recovered first from the terrible shock: "It can't be totally hopeless. The Lubavitcher Rebbe advised us to come here. If he sent us to you, then the condition is curable and you are the right person to help us."

With professional dignity and imposed patience, the doctor asked, "Is the Lubavitcher Rebbe a doctor? Did he inspect the leg?" He waved the x-ray at her. "Here, look for yourself. It's black. Nothing more can be done."

"Try something, anything. Maybe the treatment will help."

Dr. Redler agreed to experiment with some medicines and ordered Rabbi Astulin to stay in bed. The Astulins felt that he wanted to soothe their anxiety more than the leg. "If you see any improvement after two weeks, see me again," Dr. Redler said unenthusiastically.

A veteran of war, a victim of Communist harassment, and a long-time refusenik, Rabbi Astulin was not one to worry about his physical discomfort. Yet he could not conceive of missing the festive atmosphere of "770". Despite the doctor's orders, he went to shul on Rosh HaShanah and attended the *farbrengen* on the second day of *Yom Tov*. At one point during the *farbrengen* the Rebbe handed him a piece of his *challah* and said: "Eat, Reb Zalman Leib, eat — and you will recover."

Two weeks after the first appointment, on the thirteenth day of Tishrei, Rabbi Astulin went back to the doctor. Dr. Redler looked at the leg, and exclaimed in total disbelief: "It couldn't be the same leg!" He examined it again and again, shook his head, and murmured, "Impossible! This is very strange. I must take another x-ray and compare them."

There was no question. Clear white spotting appeared inside the gangrene. "I can't believe it. Healthy tissue in a blackened, decaying limb! I have never seen this in all the decades of my practice!"

Although a nurse would usually have been charged with applying the salves, massages, and bandages that Rabbi Astulin's leg required, Dr. Redler announced to his staff that he would personally attend to this case. The treatment took months, but Dr. Redler generously dismissed the high bill. Eventually, the leg healed, and the Astulin family had a private meeting with the Rebbe at *yechidus* before returning to Israel.

"You have a revived father," the Rebbe commented to one of the daughters.

Some years later, the Astulins traveled to the States again. Paying a social visit to Dr. Redler, they were sorry to hear that he had suffered a heart attack. "But don't worry," Dr. Redler reassured them smiling. "Ever since your extraordinary recovery, I have been in contact with the Rebbe and I have consulted with him on many other matters, not only medical. I don't have to tell you how helpful his advice and blessings have been."

"My first encounter with Lubavitch sounds much more like an old chassidic tale than an incidental meeting in Corevallis, Oregon," says Amiram Avital, a mechanical engineer from Kiryat Motzkin, Israel.

It was 1985, and Amiram's contract with the Israeli defense department had terminated. The Avitals spent a sabbatical year traveling throughout the States. Four weeks before returning to Israel, Mrs. Avital developed a growth in her throat.

"At first, I didn't pay much attention," recalls Mrs. Avital. "We were on vacation and I didn't want to be bothered. But the growth swelled each day and couldn't be ignored."

"I am used to functioning under tense conditions," confided Mr. Avital. "I tried to be calm as the doctors diagnosed a malignant tumor requiring an immediate operation. But I could not help but respond with shock by the doctors' refusal to assure us that the tumor could be completely removed.

"We tried to collect our thoughts. Perhaps we should fly directly to our next destination, San Francisco, where we could board a direct flight back to Israel. We would rather be at home than in Corevallis during this critical time. But the doctors insisted that the situation was urgent. We could not decide."

The next morning, as Mr. Avital was walking towards the university complex, he heard a voice calling him to stop. A bearded man with a black hat approached.

"Excuse me sir," said the man in Hebrew. "You're Jewish, aren't you? Why do you look so troubled?"

Mr. Avital's worry gave way to irritated surprise: "I beg your pardon, but whatever brings you to confront a stranger? And besides, how did you know that I am Jewish and that I speak Hebrew?"

The man was not deterred. With friendly compassion, he insisted that he share his worry with him. Amiram did not need much coaxing. Here he was, far from home, with no friends, and someone offered to lend a listening ear. He told him of his wife's illness and of their dilemma.

The man listened sympathetically, then said, "Look, someone can help you." The man told him about the Lubavitcher Rebbe, whose blessings had assisted many Jews. Amiram had heard much about Lubavitch; he remembered those friendly bearded men who had visited even the most remote army bases in Israel. But he had never had any close contact with any chassidim or with the Rebbe.

Yet, Amiram decided that he was going to give it a chance. He did not even notice that the man had slipped away.

"Incidentally," relates Mr. Avital, "I never saw that man before, nor did I ever see him again.

Ignoring the doctors' advice that they receive care locally, the Avitals were soon on line at a travel agency. "I'd like to change the stopover on our return tickets to Israel, from San Francisco to New York."

"Sorry, sir, all flights are booked until Saturday."

Amiram could not see traveling on *Shabbos* to get a blessing from the Rebbe. As he turned towards the door, the agent suddenly called him back: "Sir, you're in luck. I just located a cancellation. You can leave Oregon on Thursday and arrive in New York on Friday. Your flight to Israel departs Sunday afternoon."

"I didn't know that much about Divine Providence then, but I could not help but marvel at this coincidence, and that of the timely encounter with the mysterious bearded gentleman, or the fact that that *Shabbos* we spent in Crown Heights 'happened' to be a weekend experience offered as an "Encounter with Lubavitch" for uncommitted Jews.

"We were hosted graciously and participated in all the sessions. On Sunday, I took my place on the line to see Rebbe. I was impressed by the Rebbe's dignity, and felt calm as an inner voice told me that we had made the right decision. If anyone could help us, the Rebbe could."

When his turn came, Mr. Avital introduced himself as an Israeli officer and asked for a blessing for his wife's condition. The Rebbe handed him two dollars and said *Brochah v'hatzlachah.* He was already moving on when someone whispered loudly, "Sir, the Rebbe is beckoning you to come back."

"When are you going back to Israel?" the Rebbe asked as Mr. Avital rushed back.

"Today."

The Rebbe handed him two additional dollars: "This is for *parnossah* (earning a livelihood) in Israel."

Outside, he met his wife. "I had been standing in line for two hours," related Mrs. Avital. "When I passed by the Rebbe, I told him about the tumor and requested a blessing. He blessed me with a complete recovery and handed me an extra dollar. I went blank from nervousness, and I don't know what I said or what the Rebbe answered. Without much thought, I went right back to the end of the line.

"When I reached the Rebbe, I described my illness again, and requested a blessing. The Rebbe said, 'But I already wished you a speedy recovery. Do not worry.' He handed me another dollar and blessed me again. I cannot understand how he could have remembered me among all of those people."

Back in Israel, the Avitals went straight to a doctor, who confirmed the existence of a growth and performed an operation three days later.

The next step was critical. Was the tumor indeed malignant? Did the surgeon extract all of it? These questions could only be answered by sending a sample for laboratory analysis.

The final lab results confounded the doctors. The growth should not have been classified as a tumor and it was not malignant. They could not understand what had happened.

However, for the Avitals, this was not totally unexpected. It was part of the extraordinary logic that had characterized their ordeal.

"I still faced another problem," concluded Mr. Avital, "Although I had received a salary during my sabbatical, when I returned, I was without a job. Yet, I believed in the Rebbe's "post-scripted" blessing for a livelihood and I landed another very comfortable position in a matter of days."

"It was the winter of 1959, I had been living in Crown Heights for about two years," recalls Reb Avraham Rothenberg of Bnei Brak, Israel, "it was decades before the fax era, and overseas calls were prohibitively expensive. So by the time I heard that my father in Israel had suffered a heart attack, and he had already been in critical condition for a few days.

"I was very worried. I wrote the Rebbe in a disconnected stream of consciousness: 'I don't know what to think.'

The Rebbe replied promptly, gently, and firmly: "In similar situations, the previous Rebbeim taught: *'Tracht gut, vet zein gut*. Think positively and the outcome will be good.'

"I await good tidings," the Rebbe added.

The Rebbe's answer helped Reb Avraham pull himself together.

Three days later, after *minchah*, the Rebbe turned to Rav Avraham: "*Nu*, do you have any good news to relate?"

"Yes. I just spoke to my family in Israel and my father overcame the crisis."

"When?" inquired the Rebbe.

"This past Thursday evening."

"When did you begin to think positively?" continued the Rebbe.

"Immediately upon receiving the Rebbe's reply."

"And when was that?"

"Thursday evening."

"May such events never occur again," said the Rebbe. 'But you should always remember the importance of thinking positively."

Reb Avraham's father lived for another seventeen years.

A Belzer chassid was telling a story to some colleagues in Jerusalem. "It was one of those occasions when I sincerely missed my childhood city of Belz," he began. "After the Holocaust, I began a new life in the States. I married, had children, and opened a small business. Thank G-d, my life was relatively peaceful, until one day my daughter contracted a serious eye disease. The doctors were very pessimistic. 'She will most probably lose her eyesight,' they solemnly predicted.

"I was devastated. 'Dear G-d,' I thought to myself. 'As a youth in Belz, I knew where to turn in times of despair. But here, in America, what am I to do?'

"Suddenly, the phone rang. 'Hello, this is Rabbi Leibel Groner from the office of the Lubavitcher Rebbe. The Rebbe has informed me that you have a problem. He seemed to imply that I should invite you to come to him for help.'

"It took me a while before I could grasp what had just transpired. But I didn't wait too long. Together with my daughter, I made my way to "770" and Rabbi Groner arranged for *yechidus*. The Rebbe read my note, looked at me, and said: 'True, you have strong belief in *tzaddikim*. When seeking salvation, however, you must put your trust in G-d. Re-establish your faith in Him, renew your commitment to His commandments, and your daughter will recover.'

"I was amazed at the Rebbe's keen perception. My outward appearance resembled that of many other Orthodox American Jews. But the Rebbe was able to see that after the Holocaust, I had abandoned my faith in G-d. My trust in *tzaddikim*, however, was still embedded deeply within me by my chassidic upbringing. I contemplated the Rebbe's directives and returned to my childhood Orthodoxy. Shortly thereafter, my daughter recovered."

"I had been anxiously awaiting this message from the Rebbe's secretary. I set out for "770" immediately, eager to be able to relate the Rebbe's response to my dear sister, who had been hospitalized with suspected cancer. The doctors had not been encouraging. Some spoke of using painkillers; others recommended an operation.

"I had written a heartfelt letter to the Rebbe describing my sister's illness and hospitalization, and I felt equally emotional now as I rushed into his office. The Rebbe's reply and blessing were encouraging. 'There is no need to operate. The diagnosis is in error and your sister's condition is not grave. May she recover soon and resume a healthy life.'

"The Rebbe's secretary afforded me a moment to express my joy and relief and then said softly, "I can understand how distraught and nervous you had been when writing the letter. Nevertheless, one must always try to concentrate more when writing to the Rebbe.'

"I looked at him in question. What was the reason for this gentle reprimand?

"The secretary continued. 'If the Rebbe himself had not told me that the blessing was for your sister and that the reply was intended for you, I would never have been able to contact you. You see, in your letter you wrote all about your sister, but you forgot to state her name. You didn't sign your own name, either.'

"The Rebbe's reply prompted us to ask another doctor to check my sister's condition. His findings confirmed the Rebbe's answer."

It is not uncommon for people to contact *Chabad* Houses around the world in times of medical urgency. The Rebbe *Shlita's* advice and blessings have been known to help thousands in need. Therefore, even when a person has had little contact with *Chabad* beforehand, he may turn to *Chabad* at a time of crisis.

One day a man knocked on the door of the home of Rabbi Yechiel Lechiani in Grenoble, France. "My name is Mr. Medina," he introduced himself. "My brother-in-law is very ill. His doctors say that it is necessary to operate immediately, but they have also warned us of the risks which may result from his unstable condition. Please help me contact the Rebbe for a blessing."

The Rebbe's answer arrived rapidly. As he frequently does regarding medically-related questions, the Rebbe responded: "Take the advice of a doctor who is a friend."

Rabbi Lechiani accompanied Mr. Medina to the hospital and told the Rebbe's answer to his brother-in-law. The sick man's eyes opened wide in wonder. "Is that so?" he exclaimed in surprise. "Is that really what the Rebbe said? Only five minutes ago, one of the doctors came to see me. He looked me straight in the eye and said, 'As a doctor, I would not be able to decide whether to risk the surgery or not. However, as a friend, I'm telling you, go through with the operation!'"

The operation was successful.

This same advice was given to Rabbi Nosson Barkahan of Lod, Israel. He had been visiting his friends, the Branovers, in the town of Omer in Israel's Negev.[3] Omer is home to many highly-trained professionals. On the weekend of his visit, the Branovers introduced Rabbi Barkahan to some of their neighbors, including Dr. Berline, a world-renowned authority on kidney disease.

Rabbi Barkahan saw this as more than a casual meeting. Later he approached his hosts. "I have tell-tale symptoms of a problem with my kidney. I have put off going to a doctor because of all the red tape involved in getting appointments and undergoing tests. But perhaps your relationship with the doctor will enable me to bypass some of the bureaucracy."

Professor Branover was only too happy to assist his friend. He arranged an appointment with Doctor Berline, who discovered a large stone in Rabbi Barkahan's kidney. "The only way to remove a stone of this size is by surgery," he stated. Without

3. (Professor Branover is a prestigious scientist and his wife is a pediatrician. See page 13).

a second thought, he asked his secretary to schedule a date for the operation.

Rabbi Barkahan promptly sought the Rebbe's advice. "Act upon the advice of a doctor who is a friend," the Rebbe replied.

After pondering the matter, Rabbi Barkahan dialed the Branovers' phone number. "I wish to consult with you," he told Mrs. Branover, relating to her the Rebbe's answer. "You are a doctor and a friend."

"But I am a pediatrician!" exclaimed Mrs. Branover.

"The Rebbe said 'a doctor'," persisted Rabbi Barkahan.

"But Dr. Berline is known throughout the world as an authority on kidney disease. If he feels that an operation is necessary, I have no reason to doubt his diagnosis."

"Nevertheless," insisted Rabbi Barkahan. "Since you are a doctor and a friend, I am asking your advice."

Mrs. Branover took a deep breath and thought. "If the question was so simple, the Rebbe would not have told him to seek a second opinion."

"Look," she finally said. "You've lived with this thing for quite some time now. Why don't you wait a while longer and see what happens?"

Within a week the stone dissolved and passed naturally. Dr. Berline could not understand; neither could the Branovers or Rabbi Barkahan. But there is often an advantage in following the advice of a doctor who is a friend.

Dr. Nirken, a well-known pediatrician in Houston, Texas, made this visit without his 'little black bag.' He had not arrived at the *Chabad* House to pay a house call; this time, he was seeking personal assistance.

"I woke up one morning a month and a half ago," he explained to the *shaliach* Rabbi Shimon Lazaroff, "with a numb hand. I tried to restore sensation, but I discovered to my horror that I could not move my hand at all. For six weeks, the finest doctors in the field have been treating me, but they have not been able to determine the cause of the paralysis or to suggest any therapy. They also warned me that the paralysis may soon spread."

Rabbi Lazaroff had but one suggestion for the agitated doctor: "Why don't you write a letter to the Rebbe?"

Dr. Nirken readily agreed.

Six weeks later, the Rebbe's secretary, Rabbi Klein, called Rabbi Lazaroff. The Rebbe had three messages for Dr. Nirken:

a) The Rebbe inquired about the doctor's condition;

b) The Rebbe gave him a blessing for a complete recovery;

c) The Rebbe instructed him to check his *tefillin.*

Rabbi Klein added that the answer was given the previous night after *yechidus,* shortly before 1 AM.

Rabbi Lazaroff contacted the doctor immediately and conveyed the Rebbe's answer. Dr. Nirken could not contain his excitement. "Incredible!" he exclaimed. "Last night at 12:45 a.m. I was suddenly able to move my hand for the first time since it became paralyzed."

Rabbi Lazaroff asked the doctor if he had *tefillin.* Dr. Nirken explained that he used a pair which he had inherited from his grandfather. They had been the subject of a unique miracle: Once the doctor's house had burned down, and everything he owned was destroyed except for the *tefillin.*

Now, after hearing the Rebbe's directive, Dr. Nirken gave his *tefillin* to Rabbi Lazaroff, who flew to New York on the same day to have them checked.

That evening, the scribe called the Rabbi, "The parchment scrolls inside the *tefillin* are not kosher. In the verse,[4] 'And you shall bind them as a sign on your arm' the word, *yadecha* — 'your arm,' is missing."

The story continues several years later. Once the renowned opera singer Jan Peerce attended a *bar mitzvah* in Houston. When asked to speak a few words, he told a moving story of his own illness and recovery. Ten years previously, while in San Francisco, he had fallen critically ill. The doctors had given him no more than a few days to live.

A friend rushed to the *shaliach* in San Francisco, asking him to write to the Rebbe for a blessing. Almost immediately, the Rebbe gave Mr. Peerce a blessing for a complete recovery.

And to the amazement of the doctors, that is exactly what happened. "In gratitude," explained Mr. Peerce, "I resolved to put on *tefillin* every day.

"On his *bar mitzvah*," Mr. Peerce concluded, "a young man begins putting on *tefillin*. Let us all join him in fulfilling this practice daily."

The guests at the celebration were visibly moved. Among them was Dr. Nirken, who subsequently rose and told his own story.

It was not the lure of a new frontier that brought the Schochet family from Europe to Canada in the early 1950's. Rabbi Dov Yehudah Schochet was a distinguished Rabbi in Holland. Nevertheless, as his children grew, his concern for their education led him to immigrate to Toronto, where they could attend excellent *yeshivos* and benefit from the city's growing Torah community.

---

4.   *Deuteronomy* 6:8.

The Toronto community was quick to appreciate Rabbi Schochet's unique gifts, and he had little difficulty finding a Rabbinical post. As his home became an address for Jewish activity, their integration into the new city became easier. There were, nevertheless, considerable hardships during those first few years, such as a lack of a hot water heater and telephone.

"I particularly remember the assistance offered to our family by the Lubavitchers in Toronto," recalls Rabbi David Schochet, himself Rabbi of the Toronto Lubavitch community today. "The Lubavitchers gave much more than financial support. They played a major role in helping to fulfill the educational goals which my father had set for our family."

These chassidim shared stories of the Rebbe and his teachings with Rabbi Schochet. He was impressed, but still felt that he could not make a personal commitment to Lubavitch without more knowledge of the chassidic lifestyle.

During the holiday of Sukkos in 1952, a daughter of one of the Lubavitch families suffered from food poisoning, and her situation was quite serious. Her parents asked the Rebbe for a blessing for her recovery. The Rebbe agreed, and suggested that the parents immediately prepare a generous and joyous *kiddush* in *shul* on the coming *Shabbos*.

The *kiddush* was indeed an inspiring affair, with everyone's spirits uplifted in true chassidic joy. Rabbi Schochet participated in this *kiddush* and was both moved and mystified. "How could the parents and acquaintances of a critically ill girl manage to express such genuine good cheer?" he wondered. Soon the child recovered, and it was clear that she had suffered no permanent damage.

Less than a month after this incident, the Schochet family themselves met with similar turmoil. The Schochet's tiny one-and-a-half year old daughter overturned a huge kettle of boiling water and burned herself severely. The child was rushed to the hospital and placed in intensive care. She had suffered heavy burns on her entire body and her condition was nearly fatal. The child was quarantined for fear of infection, and even her parents were not allowed in her room.

From the hospital, Rabbi Schochet called "770". To his surprise, the Rebbe himself answered the phone. He listened patiently as Rabbi Schochet described the situation and requested a blessing. The Rebbe diverted the conversation to other matters. He inquired about the family's integration in their new place, Rabbi Schochet's Rabbinic post and other details. There was no mention of the immediate emergency. The Rebbe concluded with a token blessing and ended the conversation.

Rabbi Schochet was left stunned; no direct blessing for his daughter's recovery, only what appeared to be polite concern with his family's adjustment.

The next day, the Schochets received a message from the Rebbe's secretary. "The Rebbe has requested that you prepare a generous *kiddush* and *seudas hoda'ah* this *Shabbos* expressing your gratitude for G-d's providence with a festive meal."

This encouraging message stood in dire opposition to the grim forecasts predicted by the doctors. However, the Schochets were optimistic. Had they not themselves witnessed a precedent only a month before? "It was a very joyous *kiddush,*" recalls Rabbi David Schochet.

Days went by with the family maintaining telephone contact with the hospital three times a day from a nearby store. Suddenly, about two weeks after the accident, a police vehicle stopped in front of the Schochet's home. The officer who knocked at the door had a grave expression on his face. "We were requested to inform you that your daughter's condition has taken a sharp turn for the worse. The doctors fear that her days or perhaps hours are numbered," he said. The officer offered to drive the distraught family to the hospital.

"Only my father was allowed to enter the room," recalls Rabbi David Schochet. "When he emerged his face was ashen.

Our little sister's skin was rapidly losing color and the doctors had no hope for her survival."

Rabbi Schochet immediately contacted the Rebbe's office and described the desperate situation. The Rebbe's response was most unexpected. "Nonsense! The child is not in danger and will regain her health," the Rebbe said. He instructed the dumbstruck father to protest loudly against the hospital staff, blaming them for causing the deterioration in the child's condition.

Rabbi Schochet felt totally helpless. He was intimidated by the professional staff, who looked at him as a mere "greenhorn." Whom was he to approach? What was he to say? Evidently the Rebbe sensed his hesitation, for he repeated his instruction once again.

Slowly, the Rebbe's words sank in. Rabbi Schochet thought about the miraculous recovery of the other child only a month earlier. He did not doubt the Rebbe, and he mustered up the courage to confront the hospital staff with resolute determination. The doctors agreed to review his daughter's treatment carefully. To everyone's horror, it was discovered than an error in the I.V. dosage had caused unnecessary complications, and had endangered the child's life. The dosage was corrected and the little girl recovered. Since then, she has merited to tell the story many times to her children and her grandchildren.

Reb Chanoch Hendel Lieberman was one of the first to communicate a genuine appreciation of chassidic life in the world of art. His experiences in the Russian chassidic community were expressed through oil and canvas, bringing an awareness of Chassidism to many who would not enter a synagogue.

Reb Hendel was himself a unique picturesque personality whose constant celebration of life touched all those who came in contact with him. Up to his last days in 1976, he conducted the singing at every *farbrengen* like a true maestro, following the bidding of the Rebbe. One only had to watch his radiant face to see how he cherished this delightful role.

The overwhelming majority of Reb Hendel's paintings were of the chassidic *shtetl* in Russia. Nevertheless, during one *yechidus*, the Rebbe asked him to draw a painting depicting *Uforatza*, the Biblical term[5] meaning "you shall spread out," which is associated with Lubavitch's outreach efforts to spread Jewish consciousness.

Seeing this as a unique opportunity, Reb Hendel asked the Rebbe to explain the visual image he associated with the word.

The Rebbe told him, "Imagine a broad river with a fast-moving current. A carefully constructed dam in the midst of the river regulates the flow of the water and controls the directions to which it is diverted.

"This is the idea of *Uforatza* — to control and direct the flow of water, enabling it to reach the fields and irrigate them, and cultivate fine produce."

In 1957, Reb Hendel felt a general sense of weakness and acute stomach pains. The doctors discovered abdominal cancer. No doctor would operate, because the chances of recovery would be small. With grim solemnity, they told Reb Hendel that he had only several months to live.

Reb Hendel went to see the Rebbe. "You will recover," were the Rebbe's encouraging words.

"But Rebbe, that is totally above the natural order," Reb Hendel said. He trusted the Rebbe, but was surprised at his promise.

"Lubavitch has endured more difficult circumstances," replied the Rebbe. "Nevertheless, you must find a doctor who will perform the operation."

---

5.   *Genesis* 18:14.

Reb Hendel consulted numerous doctors, but to no avail. As each one reviewed his file and examined the X-rays, they shook their heads in refusal. In his search for a willing physician, he came across one elderly non-Jewish professor, who at first also refused. In desperation, Reb Hendel told him that he was advised to undergo the operation by the Lubavitcher Rebbe.

"The Lubavitcher Rebbe?" repeated the professor slowly. "I just read an article about him in the *New York Times*. Look, if you ask my professional opinion, I would tell you not to undergo the operation. However, the *New York Times* describes the Rebbe as having access to supernatural powers. If you're prepared to rely on those powers, then I will be prepared to perform the operation."

The complicated operation required the removal of three-quarters of his stomach. At one critical stage, the professor had a call placed to the Rebbe's office at "770": "Tell the Rebbe to activate those supernatural powers."

The secretary immediately conveyed the message to the Rebbe, who assured him that all would be well. Indeed, the operation was successful and Reb Hendel resumed a normal life. Despite the reduced size of his stomach, he was able to eat and drink normally. He lived for eighteen years after the operation, even managing an occasional *lechaim*.

The Rebbe himself once told the following story:

"A letter arrived one day from a sick man in Israel. He was scheduled to undergo a complicated operation and he requested a blessing. *Nu*, when a Jew asks for a blessing, shouldn't I help him?

"I gave him the blessing, adding that he should commit himself to putting on *tefillin* every day. The sick man resolved to do so and his condition suddenly took a sharp turn for the better. The doctors were surprised at the remarkable change. They canceled the operation and the incident became the talk of the department.

"As the word spread, many patients inquired what had caused the sudden recovery. The man told them that he began putting on *tefillin*.

"'If that's the case,' they responded, 'We will also begin performing this *mitzvah.*' And indeed, many patients began to fulfill this daily obligation diligently.

"We can see from this," concluded the Rebbe, "that the sick man's stay in the hospital was intended to bring him and others to commit themselves to putting on *tefillin*. As soon as this mission was fulfilled, he was discharged."

"Although severe heart disease had caused a permanent malfunctioning of my arteries, I was thankful to be alive," related a congregant at the Lubavitch *shul*. "The doctors had promised that medication, a restriction of activity, and other changes in my lifestyle would reduce the immediate threat to my health."

"Some time later, the Rebbe wrote me: 'Increase your involvement in the Lubavitch center's activities,' as 'this will increase G-d's blessing for a speedy and complete recovery.'

"I was taken aback. I had become accustomed to the medication and my restricted activities, which had stabilized my condition. Furthermore, the Rebbe had instructed me to *increase* my involvement in Lubavitch activity. Increase it? The doctors had so restricted me that I was hardly involved at all!

"With mixed feelings, I offered my services to the local Lubavitch center. The overburdened staff was happy to delegate responsibilities to me. As the weeks passed, my involvement grew, and I began to feel better. Soon I became extremely busy, and I neglected my doctor's strict orders for rest and minimal activity.

"In the meantime, the date of my quarterly examination arrived. As the cardiologist proceeded through the tests, I could tell that something had happened. He reviewed the results again and again, and consulted with other doctors. There was no mistake; the malfunction had corrected itself.

"Ever since, the extent of my Lubavitch activities has served as an accurate barometer for my heart condition. The more active I am, the more efficiently my heart pumps."

Reb Eliyahu Peretz graduated from *yeshivah*, married, settled in Kiryat Gat, Israel, and became attracted to the thriving Lubavitch community which had enhanced the religious life of this largely secular community.

As his connection with Lubavitch grew, he decided to write the Rebbe in order to introduce himself and to request a blessing for himself and his wife.

The blessing arrived in due time, with a word of advice: "Check your *tefillin.*"

New as he was to Lubavitch, Reb Eliyahu saw no urgency in carrying out the Rebbe's directive. Moreover, he knew that his *tefillin* had been written by a well-known, expert scribe.

About eighteen months later, on *Erev Rosh HaShanah*, Mrs. Peretz gave birth to the couple's first child. Unfortunately, the tiny boy had meningitis and was in critical condition. Weeks passed, but the baby's condition did not improve. Reb Eliyahu wrote a second letter to the Rebbe, this time including an urgent prayer for his son's health. He received the same directive he had neglected for a year and a half: "Check your *tefillin.*"

This time, Reb Eliyahu rushed his *tefillin* to an expert scribe. He looked over his shoulder as the small scroll was unrolled. The *tefillin* were written beautifully, but both men could clearly see an error. In the verse:[6] "Sanctify unto me all your firstborn..." the word 'firstborn' was missing. Shortly after the error was corrected, the boy recovered.

"Why did you come to see me?" the doctor asked Mr. David Segal with concern. Mr. Segal was a heart patient whom he had treated for several years, and his sudden visit worried the doctor.

"Please give me a full EKG and checkup," requested Mr. Segal.

"But why?" asked the doctor. "Are you feeling worse than usual?" He knew that his patient suffered constant chest pain.

"Please do the examination," Mr. Segal begged without any explanation.

The doctor shrugged agreeably. If it would make his ailing patient happy, why refuse?

After the examination, the perplexed doctor deliberated over the results. He looked at his patient, back at the results, then at his previous file and back at the patient.

"This is the second time in the last few days someone is giving me a very strange look," remarked Mr. Segal. "What's going on?" he asked, pointing at the papers.

"I don't understand," the doctor mumbled. "Your heart and your file tell two separate stories. Today, your heart is in fine condition for a person your age."

---

6.   *Exodus* 13:2.

After thanking the doctor and leaving his office, Mr. Segal thought about the first strange look he had received. It was from a scribe.

Some time earlier, Reb Shlomo Greenwald, an acquaintance who was a Lubavitcher chassid, had persuaded him to seek the Rebbe's blessing for his recovery. At first, Mr. Segal was reluctant, he had given up all hope of recovery. "When I was healthy," he argued, "I never wrote the Rebbe. Why I should I write to him now when I am ill?" Finally, he agreed to have Reb Shlomo himself write the letter. He added a short note himself stating his despair about his health.

The Rebbe's reply was short. "Check your *mezuzos.*"

The scribe unrolled the first parchment scroll of Mr. Segal's *mezuzos* and gave him a strange look. "I was told that you have heart disease, Mr. Segal," he said. "Well, so does your *mezuzah!*

The word 'heart' is missing from the verse,[7] 'And you shall love G-d, your L-rd, *with all your heart.*'"

One of my first Rabbinic posts was in Birmingham, Alabama. While living there, my curious two-year-old daughter managed to reach the container of cotton swabs and inserted one deeply into her ear," related Rabbi Moshe Stern, Rabbi of the *Shaarei Tefillah* congregation in Toronto, Canada. "We were devastated when the doctors informed us that she had apparently suffered permanent loss of hearing. She underwent two complicated, but unsuccessful operations to repair the damage. 'There is nothing more we can offer,' the specialists said.

"We asked the Rebbe for a blessing. Surprisingly, he suggested that we check our *mezuzos,* especially the one in the

---

7.   *Deuteronomy* 6:9.

child's room. Only a few weeks earlier I had purchased excellent new *mezuzos* for nearly every room in our house.

"I removed the *mezuzah*, but there was no need to have it checked professionally. The very first word, *Shema* — 'Hear' — was defective."

The Rebbe also advised us to search for a doctor in a different city to continue the treatment. We discovered a doctor of international renown in Memphis, Tennessee.

After the 'hearing' of the *mezuzah* on my daughter's door was repaired, the doctor performed an operation that enabled her own hearing to improve.

Chapter 12 —
Nerve Center for the World

Tanya[1] describes the unity of the Jewish people
by means of the classic analogy with the functioning
of the human body. Although the body is comprised
of organs of diverse structure and function, all these
components operate together as a single living
organism. By the same token, though the Jewish
people is made up of numerous individuals, each
with his own distinctive nature, it functions as a
single, vibrant unit.

Which organ contributes this sense of oneness?
— The brain. The life-energy of all the organs is
centered in the brain, each of whose components is
connected to one of the organs. Similarly, among
the Jewish people, there are comprehensive souls
whose possessors serve as nerve centers. These
singular individuals live their lives in consciousness
of others, and endeavor to tighten the connection
between them. Indeed, there are some such
individuals whose self-sacrifice for all those unnamed
others is so great, that while living in one corner of

---

1. Ch. 2. See also the *Jerusalem Talmud, Nedarim* 9:4; *Likkutei Torah* of the *Ari-Zal, Parshas Kedoshim, Taamei HaMitzvos; Likkutei Torah, Parshas Nitzavim.*

the world they can provide direction and assistance
in the remotest places.

The depth and breadth of the chassidic lifestyle has lent itself to a colorful variation of approaches. Each approach expresses a different path of serving G-d. Although this should bring about a productive symbiosis, a lack of open-mindedness sometimes leads to unnecessary antipathy.

Thus, a certain Belzer chassid developed strong views about Lubavitch and would occasionally make uncomplimentary comments about the Rebbe.

Eventually, this chassid met with tremendous disappointment. His son lost interest in Jewish practice and began to forsake his family traditions. Despite his family's efforts to dissuade him, Jewish practice no longer appealed to him.

This continued for several years. Once, this young man passed through a busy bus terminal. He was approached by a Lubavitcher chassid who invited him to put on *tefillin*. The young man shrugged. He had no desire to resume this daily practice which he had long forsaken. But the Lubavitcher chassid did not have many "clients" that day, and evidently felt the need to satisfy his sense of mission.

"Perhaps you'll reconsider," he coaxed the young man gently. "If you don't feel like doing it for yourself, then please do it as a favor for me."

The man's earnestness struck a chord in the young man's heart. "O.K." he agreed. "I'll do you a favor." The Lubavitcher was pleased. Much more important than his own sense of satisfaction was the fact that a fellow Jew had taken off a moment from his worldly concerns to develop a connection with his spiritual core.

Before he could assist the young fellow in putting on the *tefillin*, the young man had donned them himself. His lips were already murmuring the appropriate prayers. "He looks like he knows what he's doing," the *Lubavitcher* thought to himself. He was not unaccustomed to meet people in the street whose outer appearance did not reflect their knowledge of Jewish practice.

Curious, he spoke a little more to the young man who was now more relaxed and ready to talk. This encounter ultimately resulted in the young man's renewed commitment to Jewish practice.

His father was overjoyed with the turn of events, for he felt that the young man's commitment was now stronger and more motivated than before. He also felt indebted to the Lubavitchers who had befriended his estranged son. Therefore, although he had been openly critical of the Lubavitcher Rebbe in the past, he now decided to visit him and express his gratitude.

Upon meeting the Rebbe, the Belzer chassid related the events which led to his visit. The Rebbe listened, and replied: "You have experienced both the pain of a father whose son has gone astray and the great joy of his return. I feel similar pain for every Jew who is estranged from Judaism, and I experience similar feelings of happiness when he rediscovers his roots."

No wonder Rabbi Dov Ber Chein was considered a dangerous criminal in Communist Russia. Reb Berkeh's lively gait belied his advanced years; his well-worn leather satchel swung rhythmically from the cane slung over his shoulder, and most important, his sparkling eyes exuded his deep faith and chassidic soul, inspiring the generations of youngsters whom he educated.

This unique determination, matched with his skill in educating children, had classified Reb Berkeh as a prime target for the KGB. He had avoided arrest for many years, but only because of Divine Providence, ingenuity, and adeptness.

He was eventually captured by his pursuers as he attempted to slip through the Iron Curtain. After being tried and sentenced to death for counter-revolutionary activities, his death penalty was commuted to imprisonment in a desolate area.

Even after his release, one could hardly consider Reb Berkeh's lifestyle as that of a free man. He was constantly followed and spied upon by secret agents, who were only too eager to apprehend him for a 'crime' of teaching children the Torah or of arranging for the observance of Jewish law.

Hoping to distract the KGB, Reb Berkeh moved to a distant town, but its ever-present arm shadowed him even there. He went into hiding, never showing his face in daylight. Even his wife and daughter did not dare visit him by day.

Some time earlier, during his prison term, Reb Berkeh's father-in-law and two sons had managed to leave Russia for Israel. Now his father-in-law wrote, imploring them to request an exit visa for his wife and daughter. "At least they will be spared," wrote the desperate grandfather.

Reb Berkeh's wife would not hear of it. "I will not leave my husband," she wrote her father. Knowing that he could not expect to get a visa for any place other than Siberia, Reb Berkeh's father-in-law kept begging his daughter to try and save herself and the little girl.

Finally, after an extended exchange of coded letters, it was agreed that Reb Berkeh's son, who had been sent to study at "770", would ask the Rebbe if Mrs. Chein should apply for an exit visa. The Rebbe's surprising answer was that Reb Berkeh himself should make the application for the entire family, including himself. He concluded with a blessing: "May G-d help you."

Surprised, but trusting the Rebbe, his son continued asking, "Should my father present his true papers or try to obtain false ones?" The Rebbe responded with a broad smile and casual wave of the hand: "They won't realize that it's Reb Berkeh."

Reb Berkeh received word of the Rebbe's reply, and braced himself for the lengthy and nerve-racking visa application, which precisely detailed the applicant's life. Truthful responses to "Were you ever arrested?", "Imprisoned?", "For which crime?", would surely betray his identity.

To magnify the danger of his identity being discovered, he was required to submit thirty photographs together with the application. These were to be circulated among various different government offices together with the application, to check if any false information had been submitted.

The warning at the top of the application stared boldly at Reb Berkeh: For every false answer — three years' imprisonment. "That makes over eighty years," thought Reb Berkeh grimly, as the only truthful information which he proffered was the names of his family members and their present address.

The next fearful year and a half ended with a brief notice that the application was accepted. Reb Berkeh approached the visa office with trepidation. Was this a trap? True, he had filled out the application, but Mrs. Chein had delivered it and dealt with the bureaucracy. Had they used the exit visa and passport to lure him into the open? Despite these worries, the Rebbe's promise gave him confidence: "They will not realize...."

And they didn't. They handed Reb Berkeh and his family their visas and passports with bureaucratic indifference. Four hours later, the Chein family, visas in hand, was already on a plane headed for Moscow.

From Moscow, they boarded a flight to Vienna. This time the clerk was less indifferent. "Your papers are false!" he shouted. Ignoring Reb Berkeh's protests, he checked with the manager, hurling a violent curse upon 'those wretched Jews'. Soon, however, he returned with the papers. "You're lucky this time, you miserable Jews," he sneered. "The government seal is authentic."

Reb Berkeh heaved a sigh of relief and the family rushed out to the runway where the plane was preparing for takeoff. The Rebbe's blessing still resounded in his ears, "They will not realize that it's him."

"I deeply appreciated everything which the *shaliach*, Rabbi Yehudah Friedman, has done here in Canarsie, Brooklyn," relates Hertzel Borochov. "After the morning *minyan* in the *Chabad* House began to be well attended and a daily schedule of study classes proved successful, my wife, Chagit, and I resolved to obtain a *Torah* scroll for the *Chabad* House.

"Shortly afterwards, we visited Crown Heights on Sunday to mention this to the Rebbe. The Rebbe gave me his blessing and an extra dollar to put in the *tzedakah* box at the *Chabad* House in Canarsie. A while later, I spotted my wife Chagit, who had also spoken with the Rebbe. She looked baffled. 'Well, what did the Rebbe say?' I asked.

"'I don't understand,' she blurted. 'The Rebbe handed me an extra dollar to be given to *tzedakah* in... Los Angeles!'

"'Los Angeles?!' I repeated in wonder. My wife nodded.

"We were familiar enough with the Rebbe to understand that this was not a mistake. Then and there, we decided that my wife would make a trip to the West Coast. We had gone to the Rebbe in January, when the price of air travel is relatively high. So we waited a couple of weeks until the prices fell, and purchased a ticket.

"There was, however, one problem. We have no family or friends in Los Angeles, and we wondered whom we could contact to host my wife. As we were thinking, it occurred to me that on her last visit, my mother-in-law mentioned that one of her friends, Bila Allon, Chagit's kindergarten teacher from long ago, was living in Los Angeles and was involved in *Chabad* activities.

"We could not find the woman's phone number. Chagit did not want to delay the trip any longer. She was confident that I would find a place for her and promised to call me from the airport in Los Angeles.

"While my wife was on the way to her destination, I worked diligently until I located Bila's telephone number. I called, and luckily she was home.

After I introduced myself, she told me stories about my wife as a little girl, and we both spoke about our families. As our conversation continued, my wife's teacher confided in me, 'Eleven years ago, my two-year-old drowned in our swimming pool. At that time, I resolved that in the year that he would have had his *bar mitzvah*, I would have a Torah Scroll written and donated in his memory.'"

Stirred by the Divine Providence of these events, I told Bila about Chagit's encounter with the Rebbe and how she was now on her way to Los Angeles. Bila was also moved.

Some time later, a Torah scroll was donated to the *Chabad* House in Canarsie. The dedication ceremony included a guest from Los Angeles.

The telephone rang in Rabbi Ephraim Wolf's office one wintry December morning in 1969. "My boss, Israeli Minister of Immigration Mr. Lova Eliav, would like to see you," the secretary said. Rabbi Wolf, head of the Lubavitcher *yeshivah* network in *Eretz Yisrael*, gladly arranged an appointment.

"I've been considering an innovative idea," began Mr. Eliav. "Large numbers of Georgian Jews are now arriving in *Eretz Yisrael*, and more are expected. I have heard that Lubavitch has had connections with this community for decades. We are planning to build 300 new apartments in Kiryat Malachi.[2] Perhaps some Lubavitchers would be willing to settle in this community together with the new immigrants."

Rabbi Wolf responded eagerly, and the new community was planned.

Later, it became apparent that Mr. Eliav's idea was not so original.

---

2.   An Israeli city near Ashkelon.

A few months earlier, in September, Reb Avraham Tauber of Ashkelon had asked the Rebbe about his future. He had considering moving from Ashkelon, because the town only had a small religiously observant community.

The Rebbe had replied to him: "Stay in Ashkelon for now. An observant community will be established close to Ashkelon soon."

"Whenever I would go to New York," related Rabbi Yaakov Chazan, who served as a *shaliach* in Recife, Brazil, "people would ask me to deliver letters to the Rebbe for them. One year, I went for the High Holidays, and arrived just before Rosh HaShanah with a large package of letters which I gave to the Rebbe's secretary.

"The Rebbe is always very busy before the High Holy Days, and I expected to have to wait for answers. Nevertheless, just two hours after I arrived, the Rebbe's secretary contacted me.

"'The Rebbe answered one of the letters you delivered,' he said. It was for a Mrs. Muchnik who had been scheduled for an operation for a severe spinal problem. She had asked the Rebbe for a blessing.

"The Rebbe granted his blessing and added the following directives, 'Take meticulous care about the *kashrus* of your food and drink. Consult a doctor who is a friend.'

Conscious of how unusual it was to receive an answer from the Rebbe at this time, I hurried to relay the message to her. However, since I knew how difficult it was to keep a kosher home in Recife, I considered the possibility of her keeping kosher to be an even greater miracle than her hope for a full recovery.

"Evidently I had underestimated Mrs. Muchnik's willing-ness and determination. Within a relatively short time, she began to observe *kashrus*, after which her ailment also disappeared.

"Two months later, before Chanukah, I received a phone call from Mrs. Muchnik. 'I heard that you were planning a *menorah* lighting celebration,' she told me. 'My family has personal relations with the Mr. Marco Maseil, Minister of the House. If you are interested, I can arrange for him to attend.'

"Of course I was interested! Besides the President, Mr. Maseil was the most influential political figure in Brazil. No other Jewish organization had ever hosted a dignitary of such rank at any event. His participation at our *menorah* lighting would certainly be a tremendous boost to Lubavitch in Brazil.

"Well, Mrs. Muchnik did indeed arrange for Mr. Maseil to attend, and he showed a strong interest in Lubavitch activity. He was particularly impressed by the Rebbe's message to spread the awareness of the Seven Universal Laws commanded to Noah and his descendants.[3] A few months later, Mr. Maseil prevailed upon the President of Brazil to send a letter of blessing to the Rebbe in connection with his birthday on 11 Nissan.

Mr. Maseil continued his connection with Lubavitch and several years later on a visit to New York, came to see the Rebbe on a Sunday afternoon. At that time, the Rebbe asked him to deliver a speech in the Brazilian Senate regarding these Seven Universal Laws, which Mr. Maseil eagerly did.

"During the first years that I lived in Sydney, Australia," related Rabbi Chaim Gutnick, "I was contacted by the Jewish community in Adelaide. The high holidays were approaching,

---

3.   These seven laws include the prohibition against the worship of false divinities, blasphemy, murder, incest and adultery, theft, and eating flesh from living animals [and by extension other expressions of cruelty], and the obligation to establish laws and courts of justice. They are discussed by Maimonides *(Mishneh Torah, Hilchos Melachim,* chs. 9 and 10).

and their *shul* had no Rabbi. The Chief Rabbi of Sydney sent them to me, but I could not see leaving my wife and four young children alone for the holidays.

"The *Shul* committee asked the Chief Rabbi what to do. "Listen," he told them, "Rabbi Gutnick is a Lubavitcher. Write a letter to the Lubavitcher Rebbe stating that you need a Rabbi for the High Holidays. If the Rebbe tells Rabbi Gutnick to go, he will."

"I soon received a special delivery letter from the Rebbe, expressing surprise that I did not consent, and advising me to spend the High Holidays in Adelaide. At the bottom of the letter, the Rebbe added, 'While in Adelaide, concern yourself with the needs of Egyptian Jews living there.'

"I arrived in Adelaide the day before Rosh HaShanah and went to the *shul*. As I was surveying the sanctuary, a woman entered and asked me, 'Where is the most sacred part of the synagogue?' I was surprised by her question. I pointed to the *Aron HaKodesh*.

"Before I could say another word, she rushed out, led a blind teenage girl straight to the *Aron HaKodesh*, and then departed. The girl kissed the curtains of the ark and burst out in tears. She remained there for several minutes; after which the woman came back and escorted her out.

"I described the entire baffling scene to the *shul* secretary. 'Don't give it another thought,' the secretary said. She's one of the Egyptians. They don't get along with our community. Her parents don't even come to *shul* on Rosh HaShanah, so she probably decided to visit before the holiday.'

"I tried to ignore the secretary's degrading tone. All I could think of was the Rebbe's words 'concern yourself with the Egyptian Jews.' I rushed out to find the girl, but she had disappeared.

"On Rosh HaShanah, I felt the gulf between the local community and the Egyptian Jews. I tried to befriend some Egyptian Jews, and asked about the blind girl.

After the holiday, she too tried to contact me. The phone in my room rang. 'Hello, I'm Betty, the blind girl.' But an abrupt click assured me that someone was determined to keep her from speaking to me.

"On the night before Yom Kippur, I was finally able to obtain her address and phone number. My calls were fruitless, for as soon as I identified myself, the line went dead. I would not give up. Despite the late hour, I took a taxi to her home. Her family was reluctant to allow me in. 'Please,' I said, 'I have traveled a great distance, and I would like to speak with you.'

"The door opened, and I was invited to enter. Slowly, I developed their trust. After a while, the rest of the family left, and I gently asked Betty to tell me what was troubling her. In an emotional tone, she told her story:

"'My family arrived in Australia last year. They sent me to the only school in this city for the blind, a Catholic school. The people in the school are very nice, and my parents were pleased, because I had been given a full scholarship. After five months, the local priest began lecturing me about Christianity. I ignored him until he told me bluntly that I must convert. At the same time, my parents received a letter from the school: Due to lack of space in our school, we are forced to turn away prospective students of our own faith. We will agree to provide free schooling for your daughter only if she converts to Christianity.

"'One day, I overheard my agitated parents discuss the issue. They had reconciled themselves to the harsh reality that I must convert.

"'Although I know very little about our religion, I know that I am Jewish. I know that there is a G-d and I decided to pray to Him for guidance. I also knew that the Jewish holy days were approaching. On the day before Rosh HaShanah, I told my mother that I did not feel well and could not go to school. When I was alone in the house, I knocked on the door of my Gentile neighbor.

" 'Tomorrow is the Jewish New Year,' I told her. 'My parents do not attend the synagogue so I would like to ask you a favor. Please take me to the synagogue today so I can pray. I will only stay for a few minutes.' My neighbor agreed. In the synagogue, I cried and prayed to G-d to give me a sign. I returned home and waited.

" 'Guests joined us for the holiday dinner. One of them laughed at me: 'Betty! What have you been up to lately? A Rabbi from Sydney came to Adelaide and he is asking about you. How do you know him?'

I knew this was a G-d-given sign to me. I tried to call you, but my mother didn't allow it. She was afraid that you would convince me not to convert and that I would have to leave school. But somehow, I knew that you would help me.'

"The girl's parents then came in tearfully told me, 'We really don't want her to convert, but we have no choice. We are concerned about her welfare.' I promised to do my best to help them.

"The Rebbe's words echoed in my ears as I pondered what to do. I phoned the secretary of the Jewish community, told him the story, and asked him to come immediately.

"He was obviously startled by my request. "Have you gone mad?" he gasped. "It's half past midnight!"

"If you want a Rabbi for Yom Kippur, come here now," I told him. "Come in your pajamas if you must, but come."

"He arrived in twenty minutes. I told him that the community must accept the responsibility for the girl's tuition so that she would not be forced to convert. Without enthusiasm, yet with sincerity, he made the financial commitment.

"The girl continued writing to me over the years. She graduated high school with honors, went on to study in Jerusa lem, married, and now leads an exemplary religious life in *Eretz Yisrael*."

"In the winter of 1975, we moved from the United States to Europe. My wife had booked a flight from New York via Montreal, because this ticket offered a substantial saving. I was to join her along the same route three weeks later, when my job would end and our lift would be shipped.

"Before departing, we went for *yechidus*. My note to the Rebbe listed many questions about our future, including my wife's travel plans. After responding, the Rebbe added that the stopover in Montreal meant an added take-off and landing, so he suggested that we ask a doctor whether my pregnant wife should take a direct flight to Europe instead.

"Our friend, Dr. Yitzchok Diamond, a Crown Heights gynecologist, said, 'I don't see any real problem flying via Montreal. However, since the Rebbe advised you to ask a doctor's opinion, I would strongly suggest that your wife fly directly to Europe.'

"I was impressed by the doctor's implicit trust in the Rebbe, even though he was not a Lubavitcher chassid. With no further thought, my wife changed her ticket.

"Three weeks later, I boarded a plane to Montreal, where I was to meet a connecting flight to Europe. Montreal was blanketed by a severe snowstorm, and all flights to Europe were canceled.

"After waiting several hours in the airport, stranded passengers were taken by bus to a hotel in the city, where we were delayed for more than a day until the storm subsided. There was no kosher food in the hotel, and it was impossible to go out and purchase any. I had to ration my small bag of snacks.

"When we finally checked in for the connecting flight, I asked the agent at the desk, 'Are ordeals like this frequent in Montreal?'

"The agent apologized for the discomfort, and explained that delays of this nature were rare, but not totally uncommon. Then he added, 'Bad as it was, this storm is mild compared to the one we had three weeks ago! The blizzard blocked all the roads to the airport. We couldn't even get the stranded passengers to a hotel. Passengers were stretched out on the floor for two nights until the storm subsided!'

" 'Three weeks ago,' I thought to myself with curiosity. 'Do you remember the exact date,' I asked the agent.

"It was exactly the day my wife was to have landed in Montreal to make her connecting flight to Europe."

The young bearded man in the dark suit hardly resembled the regular customers of the large clothing store in a New York inner city neighborhood. But Tony, the black security guard, was not surprised to see this "regular." Every week, he would come to visit Tony's boss, the owner of the store.

"We talk about our religion," the boss had told Tony when he asked about the visitor. "He also tells me all kinds of miracle stories about this holy Rabbi of his who lives in Brooklyn and helps sick people. He has a lot of admirers, this Rabbi. I heard that even the President sends him a card on his birthday. Impressive, eh?"

But Tony wasn't thinking about the president. He thought about his own four-year-old little son, Michael, who was suffering from a developmental disorder. He did not talk, walk, or feed himself, and the doctors had been unable to help.

"It's a far out idea," Tony thought hesitantly. "But maybe...." Still, he could never bring himself to approach the bearded man.

One hot summer afternoon, Tony was standing listlessly at his post when the young man walked through the door. Maybe the intense heat gave Tony a sense of urgency. "It's now or never! I've got to ask the man to get his Rabbi to bless my son."

After waiting nervously for the man to end his meeting with the boss, Tony called out, "Hey sir, got a minute?"

The young man turned to the guard. "What can I do for you?" he answered politely.

With a what-do-I-have-to-lose shrug, Tony blurted out his request. He could see the man listening attentively and thinking as he spoke, and then he offered to help. "But there's one small condition," the young man said. Tony instinctively reached for his wallet.

"No, no," the young man said, waving his hand. "That's not what I meant." Tony was surprised. Now it was his turn to listen. The man told him about the Rebbe's campaign to begin each day with a moment of silence, meditating upon the Creator of the World and His expectations of man. He explained the Seven Universal Laws commanded to Noah[4] and his descendants which all Gentiles are obligated to observe.

"I'll write the letter about Michael to the Rebbe," the young man concluded, "but I'd like to tell him that you're trying to earn the blessing. Do the things that we spoke about for a week, and then we'll see."

"It's a deal," responded Tony enthusiastically. "I'll do my thing and you do yours. I'll think about G-d every morning and try to act right. I swear my wife will be in on this too. Next week, we write this letter to the Rabbi and you give it to him, O.K.?"

The next time they met, Tony vowed that he had kept his part of the deal. "It ain't bad, thinking about G-d and all that every morning..."

---

4.   See note on p. 166.

The letter was written, but Tony's boss left for vacation, and it was several months before the two saw each other again. When they met again, Tony greeted the young man with a flashing smile. "Unbelievable! The kid suddenly started living! He's walkin' and talkin' and he's gonna go to school this September! Listen, would you help me write a thank-you card to the Rabbi?"

Tony promised to tell all his friends about the miracle. He tried to convince them to start their day with a moment of silence and to keep those seven laws.

On the tenth of Teves, 5749, (Dec. 18, 1988), Rabbi Ephraim Shteinmetz of Caracas, Venezuela stood among the many others on line to receive a dollar from the Rebbe. The Rebbe handed him an extra dollar, instructing him to give it to *tzedakah* when he returned back to his home. "And may the country be at peace," the Rebbe added.

Rabbi Shteinmetz was very surprised at the Rebbe's comment. Venezuela had been a stable, peaceful democracy for many years. What could the Rebbe have referred to? The Rebbe's comment remained a mystery to all those who heard of it.

But not for long. Six weeks later, elections were held in Venezuela. The newly elected president enacted various unpopular reforms. Large scale demonstrations threatened the peace of the country. Now, the Rebbe's words became clear. Many anxious citizens eagerly awaited the fulfillment of the Rebbe's blessing. Shortly thereafter, the situation became more calm, and stability returned to the country.

Mr. Max Cohen from Manchester received a call from a business associate in Bangladesh. "Mr. Cohen, we've prepared a large shipment of merchandise for you. We are eagerly awaiting your arrival, so we can close the deal." Mr. Cohen was equally keen on the deal. For years, he had benefited from his association with the textile industry in that country. And yet he had mixed feelings.

He was familiar with the country. Its people suffered millions of casualties caused by civil uprisings and natural disasters such as hurricanes, floods, and earthquakes.

Only a year earlier, he had fled the country without concluding his business, after violent fighting had broken out in the streets. Some months later, *en route* from Hong Kong, he canceled a stop-over in Bangladesh because a full-force cyclone had ripped through the country.

His associates tried repeatedly to calm his fears. "Things are quiet now, Max," they reassured him. "The streets are calm and the worst is over. There's nothing to worry about."

Mr. Cohen was still not convinced. After considerable deliberation, he proceeded with the arrangements for the trip, but faxed the details of his plans to the Rebbe.

His flight was scheduled for the following Sunday. Throughout the entire week, Mr. Cohen remained in contact with "770", inquiring whether or not he had received a reply, but to no avail. Sunday morning, Mr. Cohen called the Rebbe's secretary at his home. "Is there anything you can do for me? I need an answer urgently."

"It's difficult to ask the Rebbe such matters on Sunday, because he devotes many hours to distributing dollars," the secretary said. In the evening Mr. Cohen drove to the airport. There was still time before the 10:30 PM departure. "If an answer comes, I'll be ready to go," he thought as he checked in.

While other passengers relaxed in the departure lobby, Mr. Cohen nervously called "770" several times. Friends in Crown Heights also tried to verify if there was an answer for him. In his dilemma, he called his brother-in-law, David Jaffe, for advice. After he hung up the phone, David had an idea. He hurried over to the dollar line and ask the Rebbe for a reply for his brother-in-law.

The 9 PM news reported that another cyclone had hit Bangladesh. That, and the fact that by 10 PM he had not received an answer from the Rebbe, were enough to cause Mr. Cohen to cancel his flight.

As his baggage was being removed from the plane, he placed a final call to his father-in-law, Abraham Jaffe in Manchester. "I'll have to stay overnight in London," he said. "I'll return to Manchester tomorrow." As they conversed, Mr. Cohen began to unwind and relax from the tense hours he had gone through. The men continued talking casually for a while when Mr. Jaffe heard a beep on his line. "Excuse me, Max, I have another call. I'll put you on hold for just a moment."

On the other line was his son David from Crown Heights. "I have news for Max," he said excitedly, "But I don't know how to reach him." With a quick press on the button, the elder Mr. Jaffe connected Max with a conference call. The two men listened in anticipation as David related his story.

"When I reached the Rebbe it was 5:00 PM, and already 10:00 PM in London. I described Max's situation to the Rebbe explaining that he was at the airport waiting for the Rebbe's blessing. 'It's tumultuous there,' the Rebbe replied. I ventured to tell the Rebbe that things had become calmer. The Rebbe then handed me a dollar for Max and gave him his blessing for a successful journey.

"I turned to go, but the Rebbe's attendant called me back. The Rebbe gave me another dollar and said: 'This is for the *shaliach* in Bangladesh.' I stood transfixed in amazement. 'Jews in Bangladesh?' I wondered. 'And a Lubavitch *shaliach* at that?!' The Rebbe surely noticed my absolute astonishment, for he added: 'There is a Jew in that country who is involved with Lubavitch.'

"Listen I'm going to forward the dollars by special delivery to Max's hotel in Bangladesh. I won't keep you another moment."

There was no time to lose. Laden with his suitcases that had already been deplaned, and the Rebbe's blessing, Mr. Cohen boarded in the nick of time. The long flight gave him ample time to recollect his thoughts and muse at the unbelievable chain of events. 'If David hadn't had that idea; if I hadn't called my father-in-law; if we hadn't prolonged our conversation; if David's call would have come a minute later... 'What Divine Providence.'

But what was mostly on his mind was the mysterious mission from the Rebbe to deliver a dollar to 'a Jew who is involved in Lubavitch activity.' He had traveled to Bangladesh many times. His business associates were all Moslems, and so was almost everyone else he had ever met there. A Jew in Bangladesh? A Lubavitch activist? Even if so how was he supposed to locate him in a population of 114 million...?

Upon arriving in the city of Chaitong in Eastern Bangladesh, Mr. Cohen checked into his hotel and set out to find the person for whom the Rebbe had sent the dollar.

After a two days of searching, Mr. Cohen returned to his hotel weary and frustrated. Just then he noticed a man hurrying towards the elevator before its doors closed. There was something striking in the man's face. A thought flashed through his mind. He retraced his steps towards the elevator.

"Excuse me, sir, are you Jewish?"

The man turned around and stared at Mr. Cohen. The elevator doors closed, but the man remained standing.

"Yes."

Minutes later, the two men were already deep in conversation in Mr. Cohen's hotel room. Two Jews, two worlds of business, personal concerns, and interesting experiences came together in a meeting of chance in distant Bangladesh.

Or was it chance? As they conversed, Mr. Cohen sensed that this indeed was the man he was looking for.

"The Lubavitcher Rebbe asked me to deliver a dollar to a Jew who is involved in Lubavitch activity in Bangladesh."

The man, who had introduced himself as Walter from North Carolina, was visibly moved. "Yes, I know the Lubavitcher Rebbe, and from time to time I am involved in Lubavitch activities," he said slowly. "I suppose this is the Rebbe's way of expressing his concern and encouragement to a simple Jew halfway around the globe."

And Walter began to tell his story: "My import-export business takes me to many places throughout the world, but I have spent most of my recent years in Bangladesh. Come what may, however, I always go back to North Carolina at least twice a year, for Pesach and for the High Holidays.

"Before my business brought me to Bangladesh, I was an active member of the Jewish community in Charlotte, North Carolina. We have a large community with many members, but like other communities in the States, many do not go to *shul* or observe *mitzvos*. Intermarriage is on the rise and our youth lack direction. So I wholeheartedly welcomed the young Lubavitch couple who arrived in North Carolina in 1980, Rabbi Yosef Yitzchak and Mrs. Mariasha Groner.

"I did my best to help them acclimate themselves into our community and get started with their *shlichus*. I maintain a steady relationship with them even though seven years have passed since I moved here.

"While phoning Rabbi Groner some years ago, I discussed an issue which had been on my mind. Over the years, I had met a number of Jewish families who spend extended periods of time here in Bangladesh on business. They and their children had very little, if any, connection with Jewish values and observance.

"Rabbi Groner helped me organize a Jewish education program for the children. Since then, he has been sending me educational material from North Carolina.

"Once, about three years ago, Rabbi Groner mentioned that he had included a report of my Bangladesh activities in his periodic reports of his own activities to the Rebbe."

Walter continued slowly and his next words were emotionally charged: "Don't ask me too many questions about our providential meeting here. I honestly have no rational answer, except that the Rebbe saw fit to encourage me, a distant Jew whom he heard about three years ago.

"I and all the families with whom I am involved, live in Dhaka, the capital of Bangladesh. My business affairs have always been located in the same area. I never traveled to other parts of this country *until this Monday morning*, when I felt a sudden urge to see some of the tourist attractions.

"This is how I happened to be here in Chaitong. I plan to return to Dhaka tomorrow morning."

The young newly-wed couple, Rabbi Zvi Greenblatt and his wife, Shternah, listened attentively and appreciatively to the Rebbe's many blessings for success before they left for *shli-chus* in Argentina. As he concluded, the Rebbe wished them "a good journey. May I hear good tidings." As he made these statements, he paused in thought, and then continued with emphasis. The couple wondered.

Soon thereafter, in the summer of 1978, Rabbi Greenblatt and his wife began their journey. Their flight was scheduled for a brief stopover in Chile. The passengers who were to continue to Argentina, including the Greenblatts, remained on board. Suddenly, the young couple heard their names over the plane's public address system. A port official asked them to leave the plane. Soon other travelers were also deplaned.

The couple was annoyed and reluctant to interrupt their journey; after all, their tickets and reservations were all approved. The authorities ignored their protests. When the Greenblatts expressed concern for their luggage, the authorities assured them that it would continue on the plane and would be waiting for them in Buenos Aires. Having no alternative, the Greenblatts waited for the next flight which was scheduled to leave two hours later.

As they sat in the waiting room, Rabbi Greenblatt, a native Argentinean, explained to his bewildered young wife that the flight procedures in South America can be flexible. A bribe in an official's hand can easily "adjust" the list of passengers on a plane, bumping certain passengers, and providing "available" seats on a fully booked flight.

As they were talking, the young couple heard a commotion and saw flashing red lights everywhere. Soon, they learned of the disaster they had just miraculously averted. A mechanical fault had caused a fire in the plane. Directly after take off, the plane had crashed. Many passengers were hurt and the plane was severely damaged.

Above the din and commotion, the Greenblatts could almost hear those parting words of the Rebbe — "A good journey..." In response to the Rebbe's words, "May I hear good tidings," Rabbi Greenblatt wrote the Rebbe, describing what had happened.

The Rebbe responded with a Chassidic adage, "After a fire, one becomes rich." Indeed, the insurance premium the Greenblatt's received for their luggage was sufficient to provide a down-payment on a home.

"I had taken a brief summer vacation in 1992 to visit my son and his family in Crown Heights," relates Reb Isser Kirszenberg, an employee at the Israeli embassy in Argentina. On Sunday, I joined the line at 'dollars.' As I passed by the

Rebbe, I told him I would soon be returning to Argentina. The Rebbe gave me two dollars, wishing me "Blessing and success," and a safe trip.

"As I turned to leave, I told the Rebbe that I would celebrate my birthday in two weeks. The Rebbe called me back, gave me a third dollar, and blessed me with a long life."

Mr. Kirszenberg was shocked. He did not consider himself to be an old man, and saw no reason for the Rebbe to offer such a blessing. Needless to say, despite his surprise, he appreciated the blessing.

"A month later, on a Tuesday afternoon in March, the Rebbe's blessing 'for a long life' took on a very immediate meaning. What had started out as a routine busy day at the Israeli embassy turned into tragedy when a terrorist bomb blew up the building. One wall of Mr. Kirszenberg's office collapsed entirely, and he was engulfed in clouds of smoke and gas. A photograph clearly shows the gaping hole in his office

"It is clearly nothing short of a miracle that I emerged from the shattered building without as much as a scratch," related Mr. Kirszenberg.

During the Yom Kippur War of 1973, Reb Ephraim Mol, a Lubavitcher chassid, was in an Israeli army unit that had reached the Egyptian side of the Suez Canal. Tension was high, and there was a rumor that the Egyptians would employ chemical weapons against the Israelis. Together with the rumor came an order from the Israeli High Command that the soldiers shave their beards so that their gas masks would remain airtight in the event of a chemical attack.

Reb Ephraim was reluctant to shave his beard. "It's only a rumor," he thought. He went to discuss the matter with the unit's commander. The officer respected his soldier's commitment to *halachic* issues, but he also knew that an order is an order. He allowed him several hours respite, and took the question to a higher authority. After debating, the officers agreed that Ephraim should pose the question to the Rebbe, and promised to abide by the Rebbe's advice.

From the front, Reb Ephraim contacted friends in Jerusalem, who forwarded his question to the Rebbe's office. The answer he received was direct: "The Egyptians will not use chemical weapons and there is no need to touch your beard. However, 'one must not rely on miracles,'[5] so keep a pair of scissors in your pocket, just in case."

The Rebbe also added a historical precedent. In World War II, the British had conscripted many Sikhs into their army. The Sikhs also do not shave for religious reasons. Despite the threat of chemical warfare, the British Army did not require the Sikhs to touch their beards.

In the following days, Reb Ephraim was constantly surrounded by other soldiers asking what the Rebbe had said. And indeed, chemical warfare was not employed on the Egyptian front during the Yom Kippur War.

"I first met the Rebbe *Shlita* during the lifetime of the Previous Rebbe," related Rabbi Avrohom Mordechai Hershberg, the past Chief Rabbi of Mexico. "I asked the Previous Rebbe about a Rabbinic position I was offered in Chicago. He told me to consult his son-in-law.

"I spent nearly an entire night with the Rebbe *Shlita*. Our discussion covered tractate after tractate of the Talmud, and the scope of the Rebbe's knowledge and his genius totally amazed me. From that night onward, I maintained a relationship with the Rebbe, and I have consulted with him regarding numerous personal and public matters."

---

5. *Pesachim* 64b.

In 1980, during the Iranian occupation of the American embassy, Rabbi Hershberg was scheduled to travel to Iran for a public service project. Because of the tense atmosphere at the time, many tried to persuade him to postpone his trip. The Rebbe, by contrast, encouraged him: "Go in peace," he answered. "You are certain to light the Chanukah *menorah* in Iran."

Rabbi Hershberg was puzzled by the Rebbe's closing words. He was not necessarily planning to stay in Iran for Chanukah. But if he would, there was no question that he would light a *menorah*. He did not understand the Rebbe's reference, nor the emphatic tone in his words.

Afterwards, it became clear. His mission in Iran took longer than expected, during which time he developed a relationship with some Iranian officials. He knew that there were six Jews among the hostages in the American embassy and he asked permission to light the *menorah* with them. "Just as we have granted permission for a priest to meet with the Christian hostages on their holiday," the Iranians replied, "we will allow you entry as well."

And so it was in the barricaded American embassy in Iran that Rabbi Hershberg lit the Chanukah *menorah* that year.

Afterword

The czarist government was suspicious of many of the chassidic Rebbeim and open to hear any charges leveled against them. Thus when an accusation was leveled against R. Yisrael of Ruzhin, they promptly imprisoned him, and planned to exile him to Siberia.

Craft, boldness, and many thousands of rubles enabled R. Yisrael's chassidim to kidnap their Rebbe from his captors and have him transferred over the border to Hungary where he settled in the town of Sadiger.

His chassidim in the Ukraine were of course happy, for their Rebbe was now able to live freely, but also sad, for there were strict restrictions against crossing the border, and the chances of their ever seeing him again were few.

One chassid thought of an idea. He was a wholesale textile merchant and had business connections with dealers in many countries.

He came to the Russian government with a proposal. There was a fair in Vienna where fine fabrics that were not usually available in Russia would be sold. He would go to Vienna, purchase a large quantity of these fabrics, import them to Russia, pay full customs duty on them, and sell them to the dress-conscious Russian aristocrats.

"Everyone will profit," he explained. "The nobles will have fine clothes; you will profit from the customs duty; and there will still be enough left for me to make it worth my while."

The Russians were eager to make the money, but reluctant to relax their travel restrictions. "What is the minimum time you need for this enterprise?" they asked.

"A week," the chassid answered.

"We will grant you an exit visa for a week, but no longer," the Russians said.

Beyond the profit he could make, the chassid of course had another motive for his trip. From Vienna, he could travel to Sadiger for *Shabbos.*

After completing his purchases in Vienna and dispatching them to Russia, he headed to Sadiger, arriving mid-Friday afternoon. He was an experienced chassid, and knew how to appreciate a *Shabbos* with his Rebbe. He gratefully soaked in the *davenning*,[1] the *tish*,[2] and the teachings of the Rebbe, making sure that they remained boldly imprinted within his memory. All to soon, the *Shabbos* was over.

On Saturday night, before he departed, he took leave of Reb Yisrael at a private meeting. After telling the Rebbe about the chassidim in the Ukraine and asking for blessings for his own personal affairs, he made a special request.

"I don't know when, if ever, I will have the opportunity of spending another *Shabbos* with the Rebbe," he said. "Could the Rebbe perhaps give me something, a coin or a sacred article, share with me a teaching, or advise me to keep a practice, which will enable me to keep alive the connection between us?"

Reb Yisrael surprised the chassid with the immediacy of his response. "I have a message for you, for all my chassidim in the Ukraine, and in a larger sense, for all Jews.

"Despite the difficulties confronting the Jews at present, we have the solace that the overwhelming majority of our people hold true to our Torah heritage. This will not always be the case. An age is coming when those who observe the Torah will be in the minority, and most of our people will be unaware of their roots.

"And there will be heavenly signs which will appear to lead people away from the Torah. If the prophet Elijah would conduct his confrontation with the idolatrous prophets of the Baal[3] in that future era, the fire would descend, not on the altar built for G-d, but on the altar of the Baal.

---

1. Yid.: "prayers".
2. Yid.: "table"; i.e., the ceremonial Sabbath meal which a chassidic Rebbe conducts in the company of his chassidim.
3. *I Kings* 18:17-40.

"What will give our people the strength to endure the challenges of that era? — Coming together and exchanging stories of *tzaddikim*, enlightening stories of righteous men. Joining together — in their families, with their friends, and in their communities — and relating stories of *tzaddikim* will inspire our people and empower them to bring about the coming of *Mashiach*."

* * *

In one of his letters[4] the Lubavitcher Rebbe *Shlita* writes, "From the days when I first began attending *cheder*, and even before then, I began to picture the Future Redemption in my mind."

In the first *chassidic* discourse the Rebbe delivered after assuming the leadership of the *Chabad* movement,[5] he outlined his goals for our generation:

> We are in the midst of the period called *(ikvesa diMeshicha* (the time when the approaching footsteps of *Mashiach* can be heard). Indeed, we are at the conclusion of this period. Our task is to complete the process of drawing down the Divine Presence... so that it should abide within our world.

In the talks he delivered on the same occasion,[6] the Rebbe explained that though Moshe could have constructed the entire Sanctuary himself, he refrained from doing so, in order to enable the entire Jewish people to participate in this endeavor. Similarly, the Rebbe continued, the Rebbeim of past generations did not want the campaign to bring *Mashiach* to be their private undertaking, but rather an effort shared by the Jewish people as a whole, and by every individual Jew.

This has been the center of Lubavitch attention throughout the four decades of the Rebbe's leadership to date, and especially so, since the eve of the 28th of Nissan, 5751. On that

---

4. *Igros Kodesh* (Letters) of the Rebbe *Shlita*, Vol. 12, p. 414.
5. *Basi LeGani 5711* (English translation; Kehot, N.Y., 1990), sec. 3.
6. *Likkutei Sichos*, Vol. II, p. 501.

evening, the Rebbe turned to his followers with a cry from the heart:[7]

> What more can I do to motivate the entire Jewish people to clamor and cry out, and thus actually bring about the coming of *Mashiach?*... All that I can possibly do is give the matter over to you. Now, do everything you can do to bring *Mashiach,* here and now, immediately.... I have done whatever I can; from now on you must do whatever you can.

* * *

In Lubavitch, every chassidic story has always been considered a teaching, and chassidim have always tried to pinpoint the lessons that could be derived from it. Beyond all the particular lessons that can be derived from this collection of stories of the Rebbe *Shlita,* it is our hope that it will motivate our readers to join in shouldering the task that the Rebbe *Shlita* has identified as of utmost immediate relevance — making the world conscious of *Mashiach* and creating an environment in which his mission can be fulfilled.[8]

---

7.   *Sound the Great Shofar* (Kehot, N.Y., 1992), pp. 35-36.

8.   *Ibid.,* p. 113.

Glossary

An asterisk indicates a cross reference within this Glossary.
All non-English entries are Hebrew unless otherwise indicated.

"770": 770 Eastern Parkway, the address of Lubavitch World Head-quarters today

Adar: the twelfth month of the Jewish year when counting from Nis-san (or the sixth when counting from Tishrei); the month of joy and celebration in which the holiday of Purim is celebrated

afikoman: the piece of the middle *matzah** which is broken at the beginning of the Pesach *Seder,** hidden throughout the recitation of the *Haggadah,* and eaten at the conclusion of the festive meal

aliyah (lit., "ascent"): immigration to *Eretz Yisrael*

Aron HaKodesh (lit., "the holy ark"): the place where the Torah scrolls are held in a synagogue

Asiyah (lit., "action"), the World of: the lowest of the four spiritual worlds

Atzilus (lit., "emanation"), the World of: the highest of the four spiritual worlds, the world which is in a state of infinity, but nevertheless, contains entities whose nature is defined

bris: (lit., "covenant"): referring to the covenant of circumcision

Chabad (acronym for the Hebrew words meaning "wisdom, understanding, and knowledge"): the approach to Chassidism which filters its spiritual and emotional power through the intellect; a synonym for *Chabad* is **Lubavitch,* the name of the town where this movement originally flourished

Chabad House: An outreach center established by the *Chabad* movement

challah: a loaf of fine bread baked in honor of the Sabbath and festivals

Chanukah (lit., "dedication"): eight-day festival beginning 25 Kislev, commemorating the Maccabees' rededication of the Temple in the second century B.C.E., and marked by the kindling of lights chassid: (a) adherent of the Chassidic movement; (b) follower of a Rebbe

Chassidus: chassidic thought

cheder (pl., *chadarim*): school in which young children learn reading skills and begin the study of the Torah

chol hamoed: The intermediate days of a festival

chutzpah: nerve

davenning (Yid.): "prayers".

erev: the day preceding

Elul: the sixth month of the Jewish year when counting from Nissan (or the twelfth when counting from Tishrei); a month devoted to repentance and soul-searching in preparation for the Days of Awe

emunah: faith

Eretz Yisrael: the Land of Israel

farbrengen: a gathering of chassidim

gabbai: the person responsible for the proper functioning of a synagogue or communal body

gartel: prayer belt

gemach: an acronym for the Hebrew words *gemilus chesed* which mean "deed of kindness," a term used for an interest-free loan, or for a fund which distributes such loans

halachah (pl., *halachos*): (a) the body of Torah law; (b) a particular law

Havdalah: (lit., "distinction"): the blessings recited over a cup at the conclusion of a Sabbath or festival to distinguish it from the ordinary weekdays that follow

ikvesa diMeshicha (Aram.): the time when the approaching footsteps of *Mashiach* can be heard

kashrus: the state of being kosher*

kiddush (lit., "sanctification"): (a) the blessing over the wine expressing the sanctity of the Sabbath or of a festival; (b) refreshments served in the synagogue after the recital of *kiddush*, the occasion is usually graced by the sharing of Torah thoughts and song

Kiddush Levanah (lit., "the sanctification of the moon"): a group of prayers recited in the first half of each month blessing the new moon

kohen: priests, the descendants of Aaron

kosher (lit., "fit for use"): an adjective used to indicate that food or religious articles have met the standards Torah law prescribes for their use

lechaim (lit., "to life"): the toast offered over strong drink

maamar: a Chassidic discourse

maariv: the evening prayer service

machzor: the special prayer book used on holidays

Mashiach (lit., "the anointed one"): the Messiah

mashpia (lit., "source of influence"): a spiritual mentor serving in a *yeshivah** or a chassidic community

matzah (pl., *matzos*): the unleavened bread eaten on Passover

mechitzah (lit., "partition"): the partition separating between the men's and women's sections in a synagogue.

Mem: The thirteenth letter of the Hebrew alphabet

menorah: The candelabra in the Temple; the term is also used to refer to the candelabra lit on Chanukah

mezuzah (pl., *mezuzos;* lit., "doorpost"): a small parchment scroll affixed to a doorpost which contains the first two paragraphs of the *Shema* (Deuteronomy 6:4-9 and 11:13-21)

mikveh (pl., *mikvaos*): a ritual bath used by women for purification after emerging from the state of *niddah,* and used by both men and women in their endeavors to attain spiritual self-refinement

minchah: the afternoon prayer service

minyan (lit., "number"): the quorum necessary for prayer

mitzvah (pl., *mitzvos;* lit., "command"): a religious obligation; one of the Torah's 613 Commandments

Moshe Rabbeinu: Moses our teacher

nadden: dowry

Negev: the southern portion of *Eretz Yisrael**

nigleh (lit., "the revealed [knowledge]"): the study of the Jewish law as reflected in the Talmud, and in the works of the subsequent commentaries and codifiers

nistar (lit., "the hidden knowledge"): the Jewish mystic tradition, also known as the *Kabbalah*

Nissan: the first month of the Jewish year according to certain reckonings, or the seventh when counting the months from Tishrei; the month of the Exodus from Egypt

Pesach: Passover, seven-day (eight in the diaspora) festival beginning on 15 Nissan, commemorating the Exodus from Egypt

Pesach Sheni (lit., "the second Passover"): opportunity given to certain persons who were unable to offer the Paschal sacrifice to do so one month later, on 14 Iyar

Purim (lit., "lots"): one-day festival falling on 14 Adar and commemorating the miraculous salvation of the Jews of the Persian Empire in the fourth century B.C.E.

Rambam (acronym for Rabbi Moshe ben Maimon; 1135-1204): Maimonides, one of the foremost Jewish thinkers of the Middle Ages; his *Mishneh Torah* is one of the pillars of Jewish law, and his *Guide to the Perplexed*, one of the classics of Jewish philosophy

Rashi (acronym for Rabbi Shlomo Yitzchaki; 1040-1105): The sage whose commentaries on the Torah and the Talmud are regarded as the classic guides to these texts.

rav (lit., "Rabbi"): the *halachic* authority and spiritual guide of a community

Reb (Yid.): for Mr.

Rebbe (lit., "my teacher [or master]"): saintly Torah leader who serves as spiritual guide to a following of chassidim

Rebbitzin: the wife of a Rabbi or Rebbe

Rosh HaShanah (lit., "head of the year"): the New Year festival, falling on 1 and 2 Tishrei

Rosh Yeshivah (lit. "head of the academy"): an academic leader of a *yeshivah**

Seder (lit., "order"): the order of service observed at home on the first two nights of Passover (see *Pesach)

shaliach (lit., "agent"): an emissary of the Lubavitcher Rebbe *Shlita** involved in Jewish outreach work

Shabbos: the Sabbath

Shavuos (lit., "weeks"): festival commemorating the Giving of the Torah at Sinai, in *Eretz Yisrael* falling on 6 Sivan, and in the Diaspora on 6-7 Sivan

Shlita: an acronym for the Hebrew words meaning: "May he live a long and good life"

shochet: ritual slaughterer

shomer-Shabbos: Sabbath observant

shul: synagogue

shtetl (Yid. "village"): the Eastern European townships where many Jews lived in the previous centuries

Simchas Torah (lit., "the rejoicing of the Torah"): the final day (in *Eretz Yisrael*, the eighth day; in the diaspora, the ninth) of the festival of Sukkos on which the annual cycle of Torah readings is completed; this event is celebrated with exuberant rejoicing

Sivan: the third month of the Jewish year when counting from Nissan (or the ninth when counting from Tishrei)

Sukkos (lit., "Booths"): seven-day festival (eight days in the Diaspora) beginning on 15 Tishrei, taking its name from the temporary dwelling in which one lives during this period

Talmud: the basic compendium of Jewish law, thought, and Biblical commentary; when unspecified refers to the *Babylonian Talmud* authored in Mesopotamia at the end of the fifth century C.E.

Tammuz: the fourth month of the Jewish year when counting from Nissan (or the tenth when counting from Tishrei)

Tanya: the classic text of **Chabad* chassidic thought authored by the Alter Rebbe

tefillin: small black leather cubes containing parchment scrolls inscribed with the *Shema* and other Biblical passages; bound to the head and forearm, customarily worn by men during the morning prayer service

tish (Yid.): "table"; i.e., the ceremonial Sabbath meal which a chassidic Rebbe conducts in the company of his chassidim

Tishrei: the first month of the Jewish year according to certain reckonings, or the seventh when counting the months from Nissan; the month which includes **Rosh HaShanah, *Yom Kippur and *Sukkos

Teves: the tenth month of the Jewish year when counting from Nissan (or the fourth when counting from Tishrei)

tzaddik, pl. *tzaddikim:* righteous man, often used as a synonym for Rebbe

tzedakah: charity

Uforatza (lit., "and you shall spread out"): the Biblical phrase that has become a byline for Lubavitch outreach efforts

Yasher Koach: a term used to imply both congratulations and thanks

yechidah: the highest of the five levels of the soul, the rung in which the soul is united in absolute unity with G-d

yechidus: a private meeting with a Rebbe

yeshivah, pl. *yeshivos:* Rabbinical academy

Yid (Yid.): Jew

Yom Kippur: the Day of Atonement, fast day falling on 10 Tishrei and climaxing the Days of Awe

Yud-Beis Tammuz: the twelfth of Tammuz; the Previous Rebbe's birthday and the anniversary of his release from capital sentence and imprisonment in Soviet Russia in 1927

Yud Shvat (lit., "the Tenth of Shvat"): anniversary of the passing of the *Previous Rebbe in 1950

Yud-Tes Kislev (lit., "the Nineteenth of Kislev"): anniversary of the passing of the Maggid of Mezritch in 1772, and anniversary of the release from capital sentence of his disciple, the *Alter Rebbe, in 1798

לזכות
ב"ק אדמו"ר מלך המשיח שליט"א
May the Torah and the prayers
of the tens of thousands of adults and children
who have learned to study and to pray
through the inspiration of the Rebbe *Shlita*
stand him now in good stead,
and may we be soon privileged once again
to hear from his lips
with ever-increasing vigor and joy
the long-awaited Torah teachings
of the Days of *Mashiach*.

& in honor of
Shalom שיחי׳
On the occasion of his Bar Mitzvah
24th Day of Tishrei, 5754

& in honor of his brothers & sister
**Yaakov Yitzchak, Rachel, Yosef,
Yehuda Tzvi, Binyamin Meir
& Yonatan Dovid** שיחיו

dedicated by their parents
Mr. & Mrs. Nachum & Sorel שיחיו
Eizicovics

& grandparents
Mr. & Mrs. Sol שיחיו **Sherman**
Mrs. Leah שתחי׳ **Eizicovics**

(Thornhill, Ontario)